Art Coloring Book for Adults
Edgar Degas

Sheila Dunn

About Edgar Degas

Edgar Degas was born Hilaire-Germain-Edgar De Gas in 1834 in Paris. His middle class family had changed the spelling of their last name from Degas to "de Gas" to appear aristocratic. As an adult, Edgar reverted to the original spelling of his surname. His family had an appreciation for music. His mother was an opera singer. Musicians were invited to perform in the family home.

His most popular work includes pastel paintings of ballerinas and race horses. He often used female models for his drawing sessions. In addition to pastel paintings, Degas created oil paintings and sculptures. Though the art of Edgar Degas exemplifies many of the characteristics of the impressionists of the day such as Manet, Degas never accepted being labeled as an impressionist. His freedom in the use of color is similar to the impressionists. However, he preferred to be known as a realist.

Degas believed that artists must live alone. He never married. Degas was friends with a group of artists including Manet, Sisley, Monet, and Renior. They would often meet at the Café Guerbois. Edgar Degas received much respect and notoriety during his lifetime. He promoted his work throughout his twilight years. Degas died in 1917 at the age of 83.

Art Coloring Books for Adults

These art coloring books created by Sheila Dunn feature a color photo of popular artwork on the left and a grayscale version on the right. Challenge yourself to copy the color image exactly or color the artwork any way you like. Due to the way color images are treated by printers, all the paper has a semi-gloss finish. If you prefer to color on a matte surface paper like regular printer paper or cardstock, you may scan and print the grayscale images.

When coloring a grayscale image, you may want to use light layers of color allowing the grayscale shading to show. This produces a sense of depth in the colored image. Another approach is the use the grayscale photo as a guide to using different shades of the same color of markers, gel pens, or other mediums to show shading in that way. Coloring grayscale is a fun way to practice adding depth and dimension to your colored pages. I hope you enjoy this book. If you would like more information about my original artwork or coloring books, please visit NewDayDrawings.com. I invite you to share photos of pages you colored from my books. I'd love to see your work!

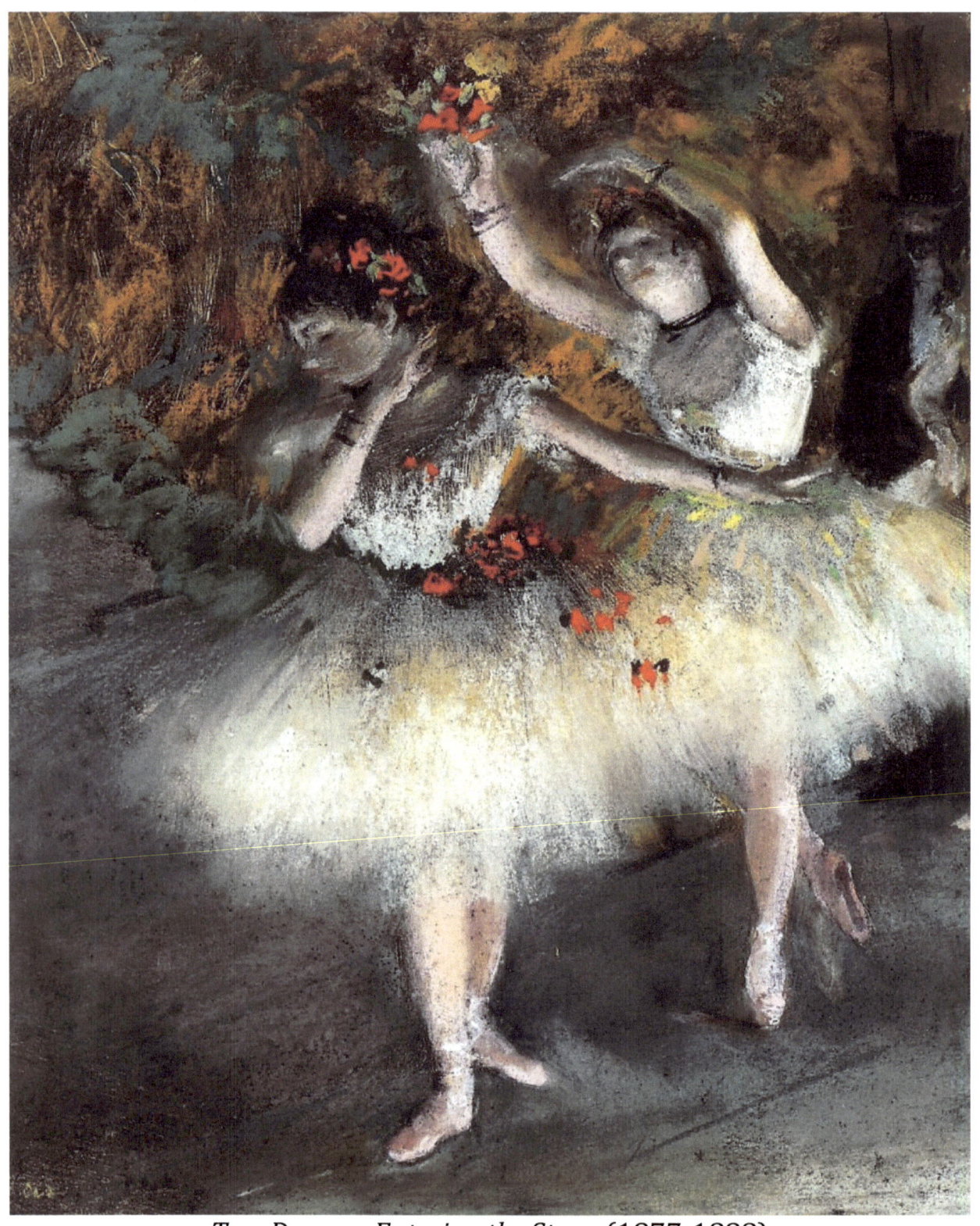

Two Dancers Entering the Stage (1877-1888)
Edgar Degas

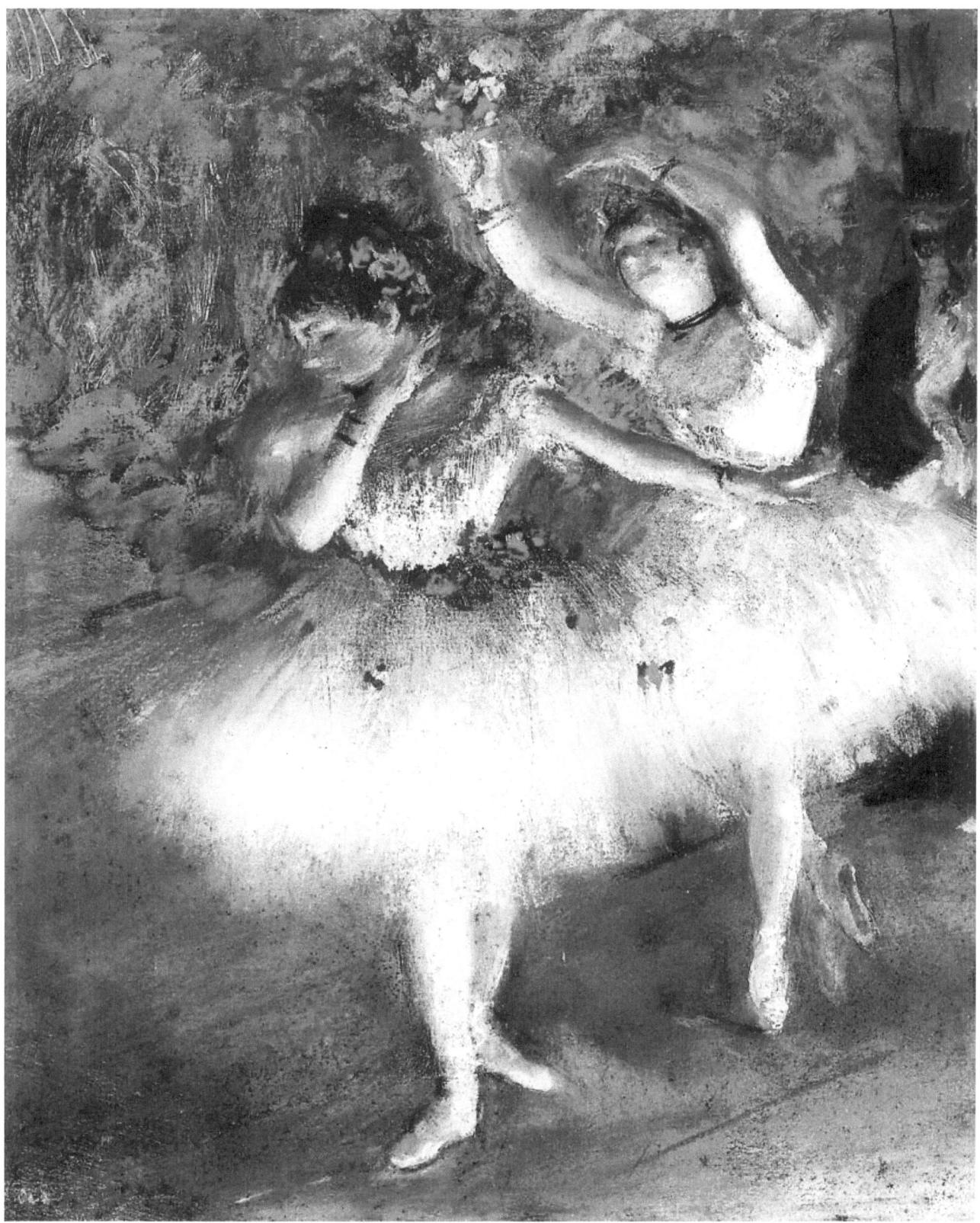

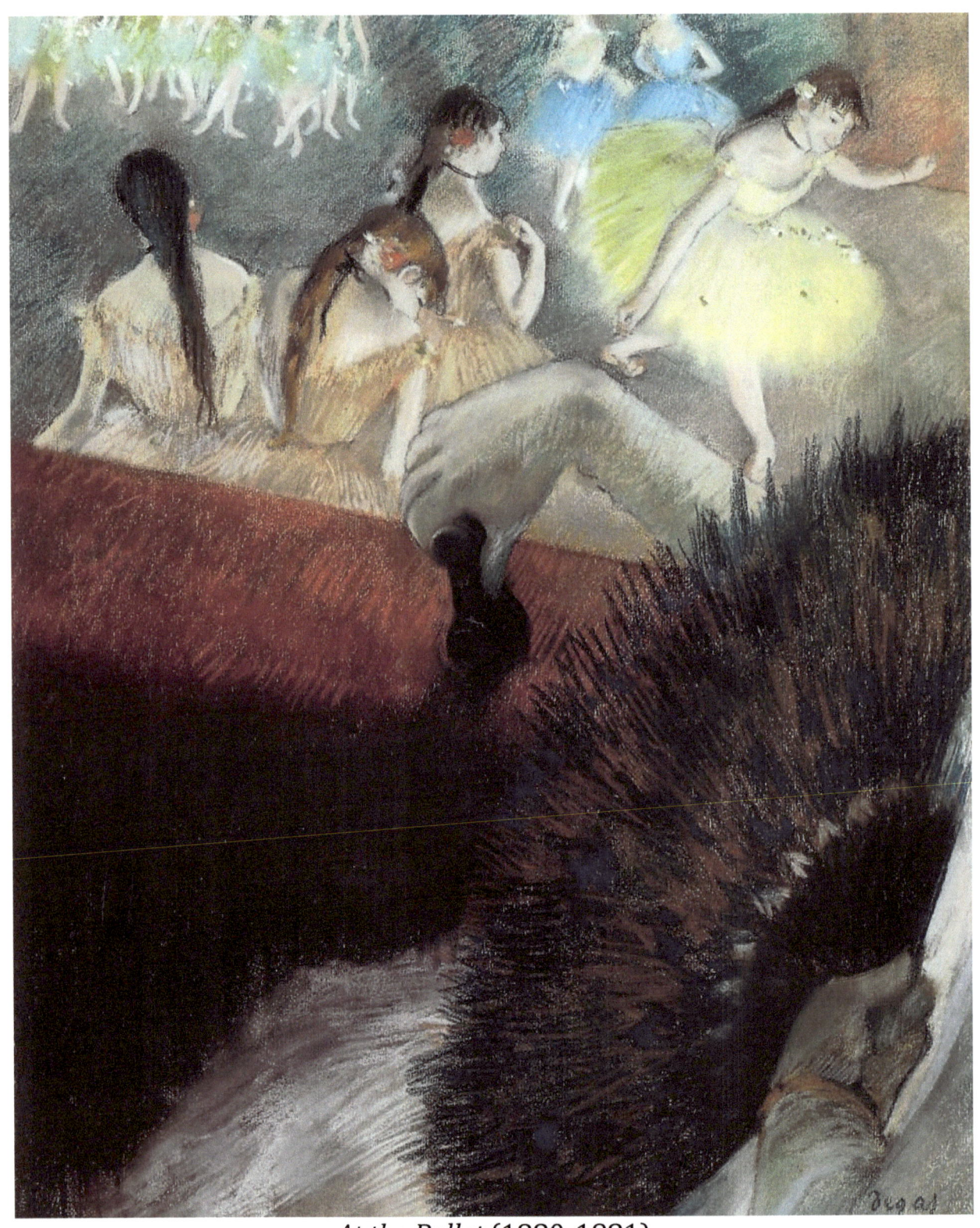

At the Ballet (1880-1881)
Edgar Degas

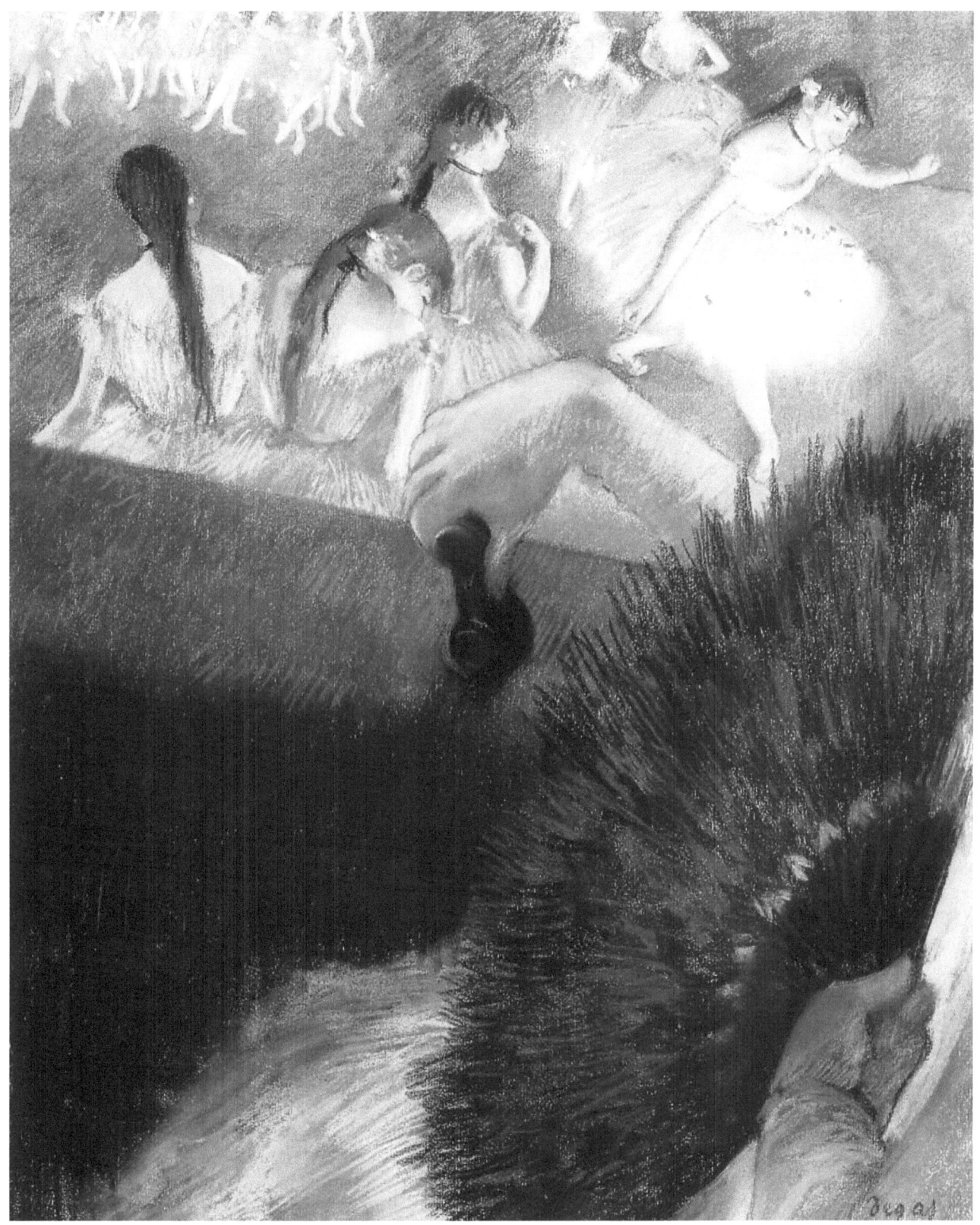

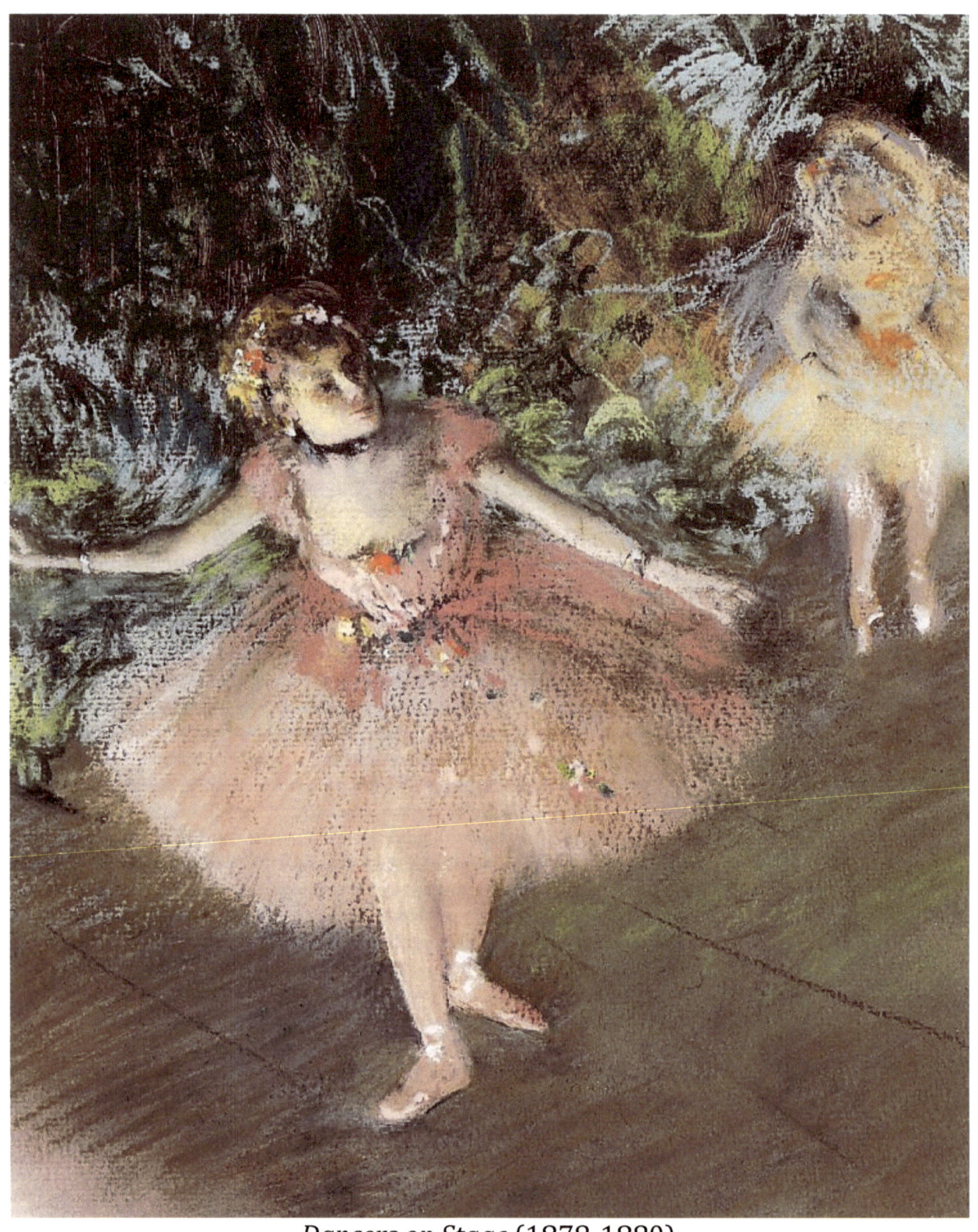

Dancers on Stage (1878-1880)
Edgar Degas

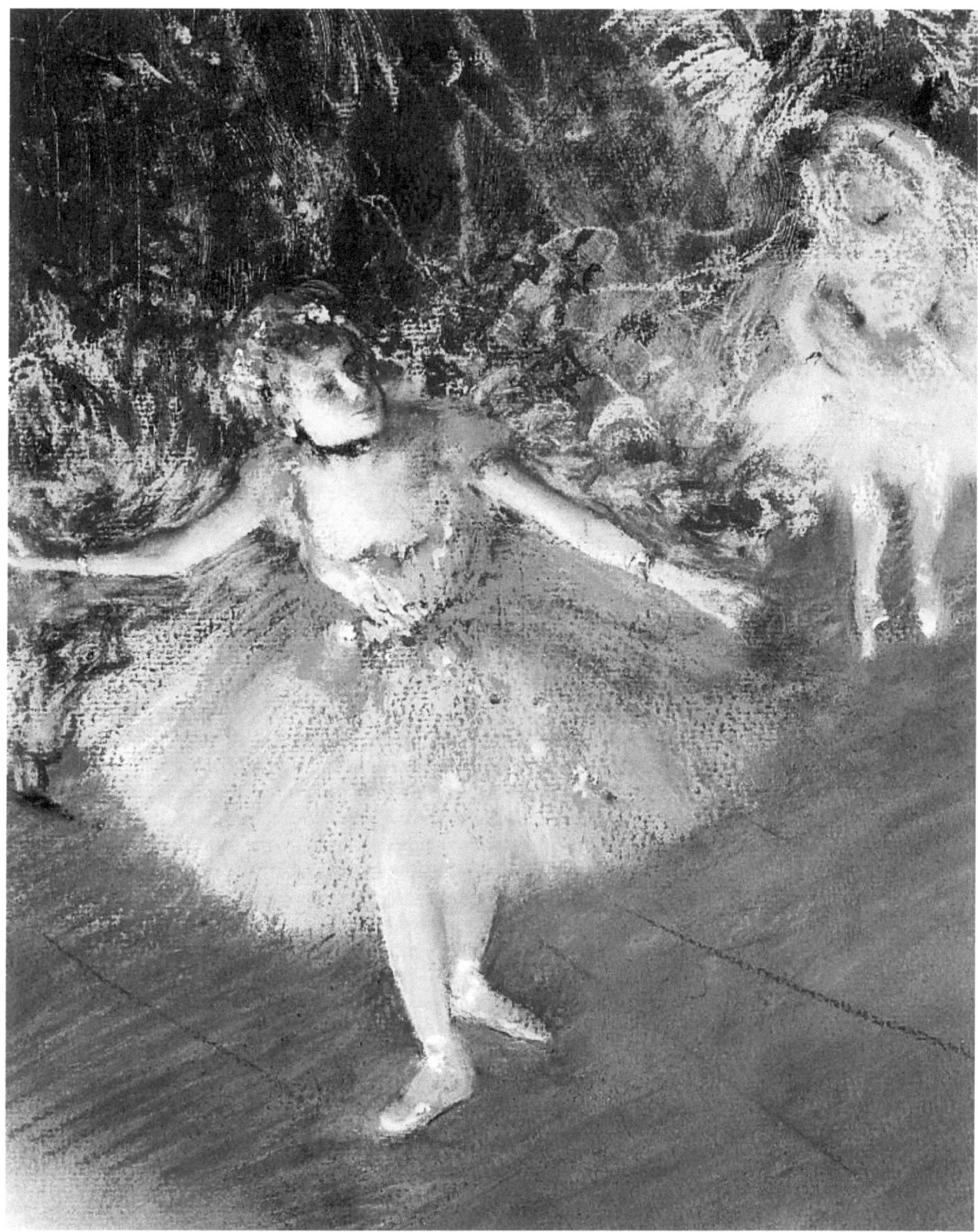

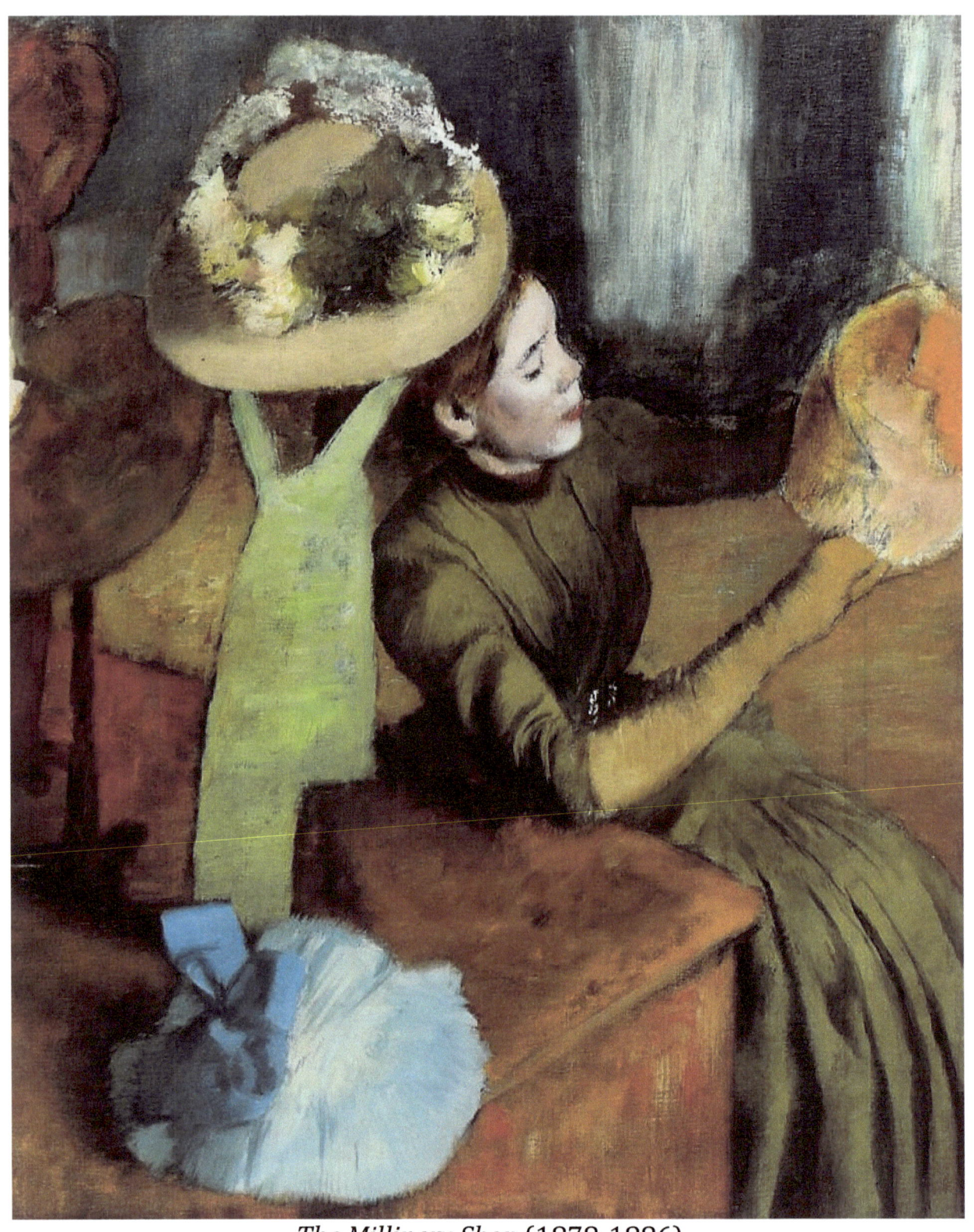

The Millinery Shop (1878-1886)
Edgar Degas

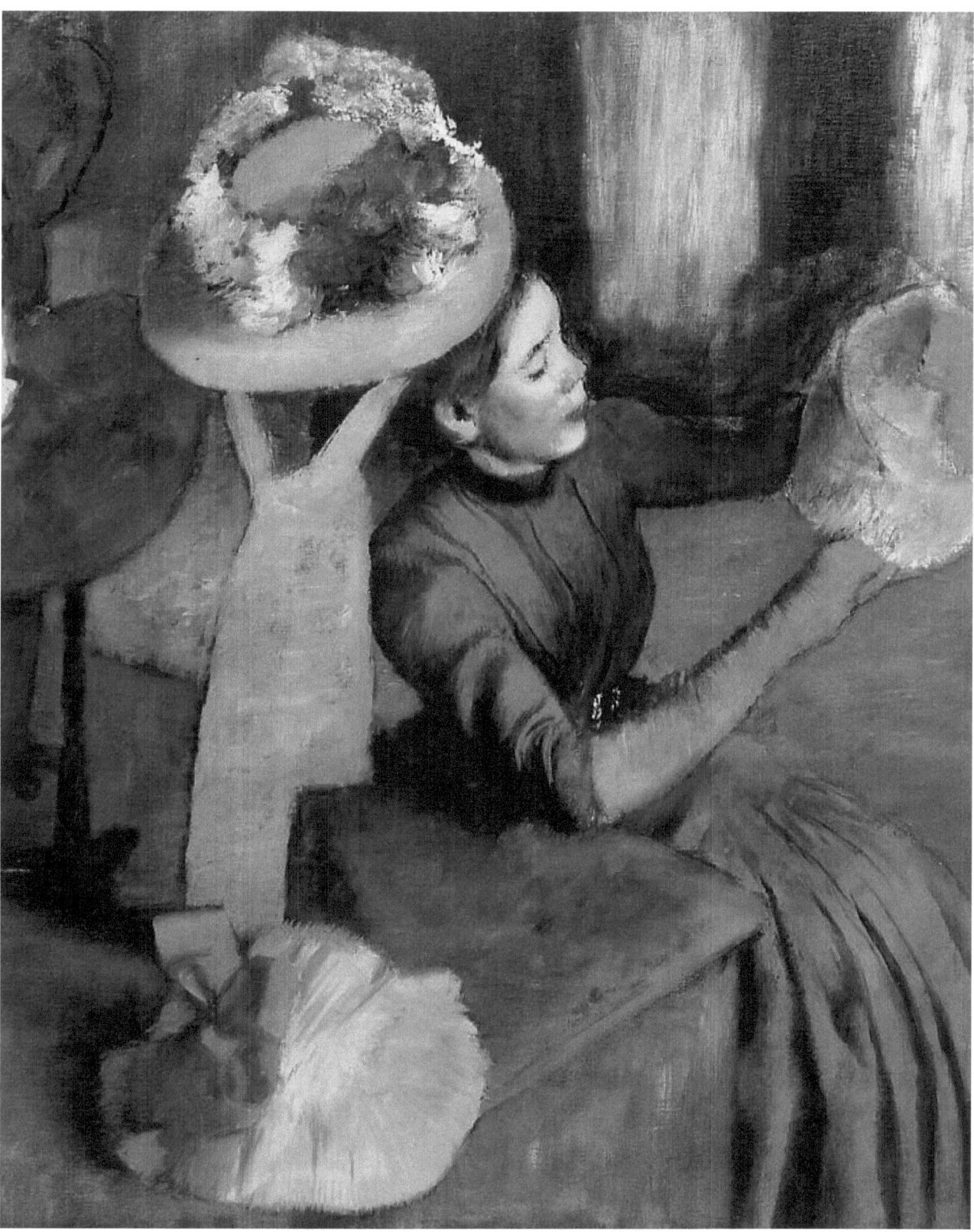

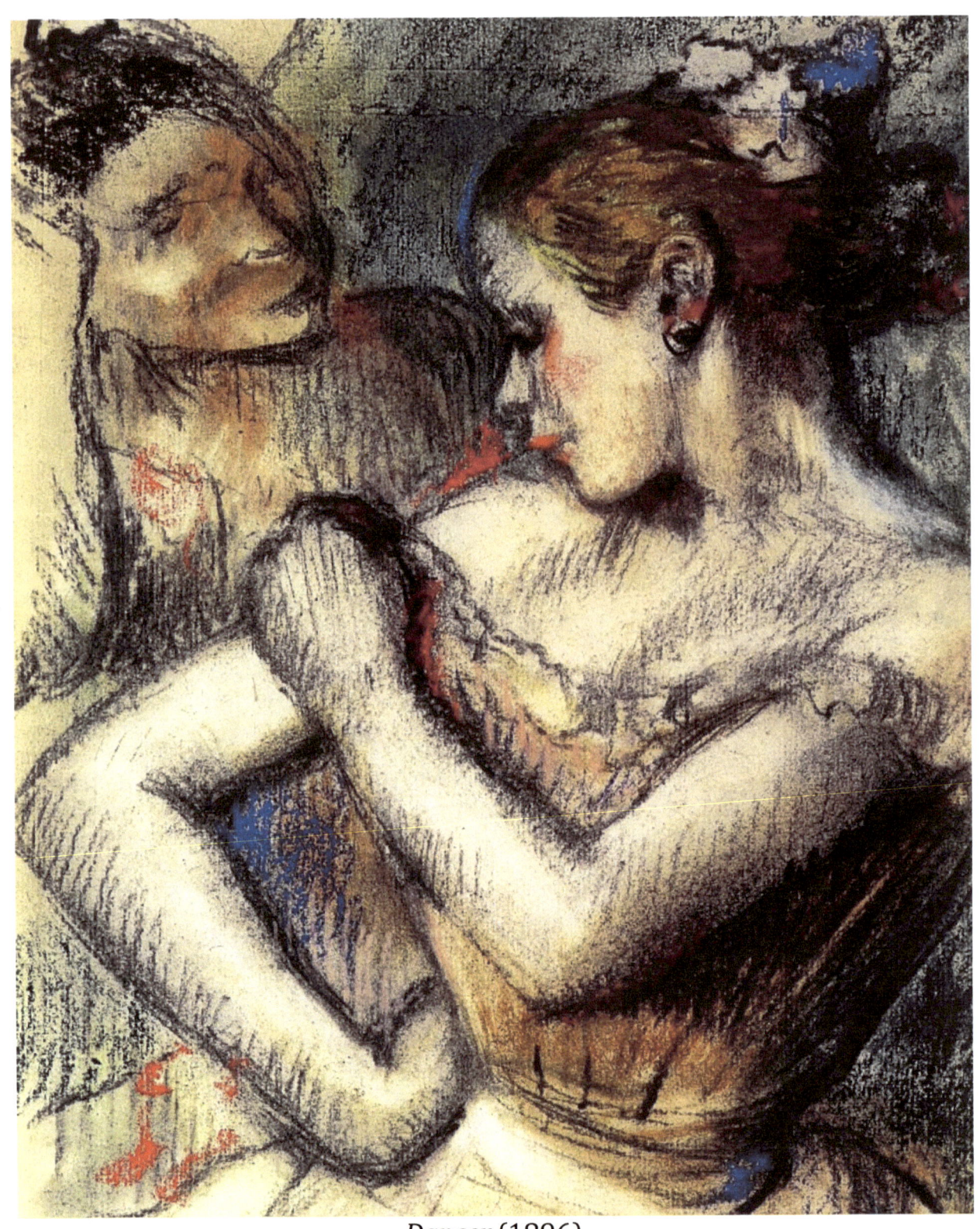

Dancer (1896)
Edgar Degas

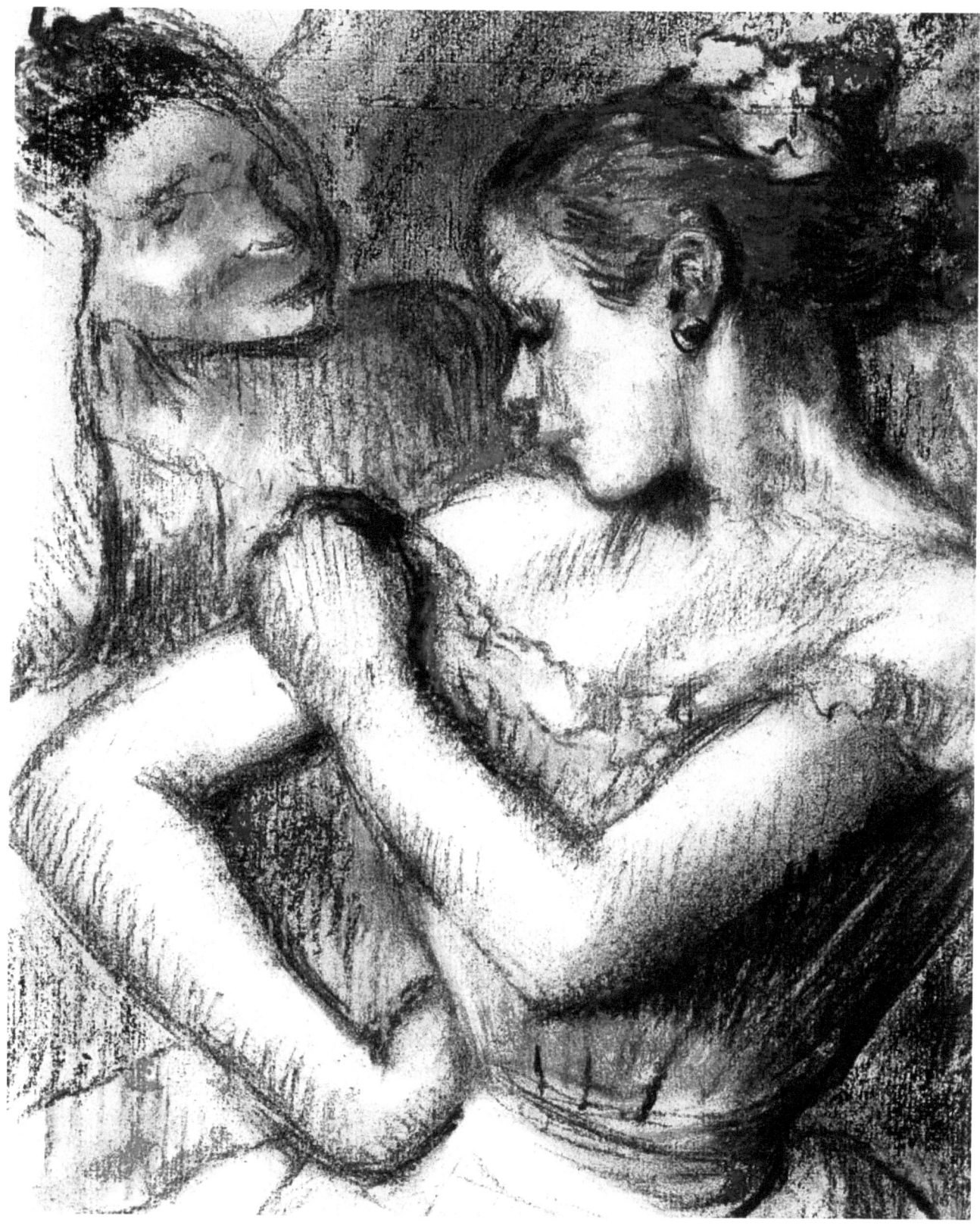

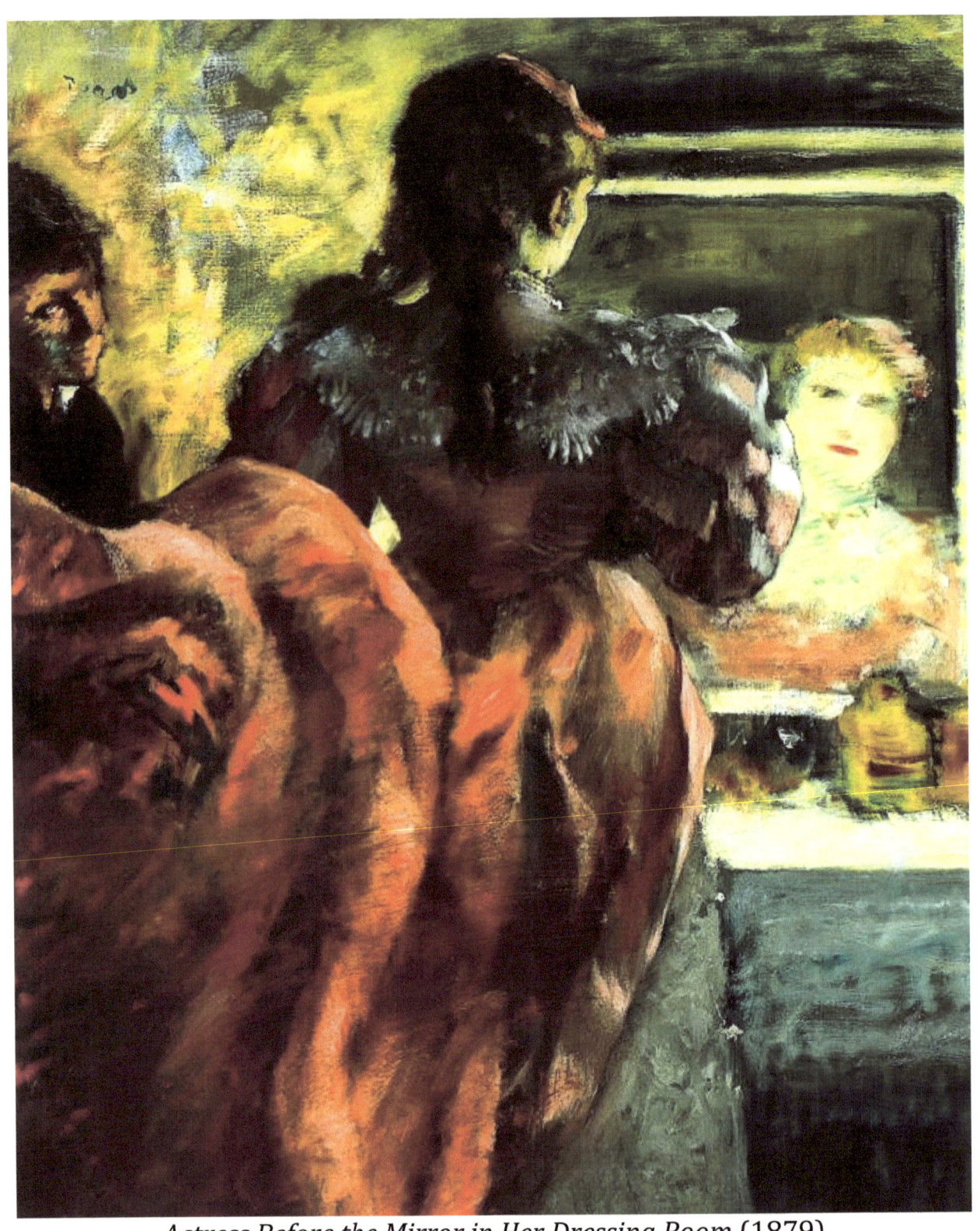

Actress Before the Mirror in Her Dressing Room (1879)
Edgar Degas

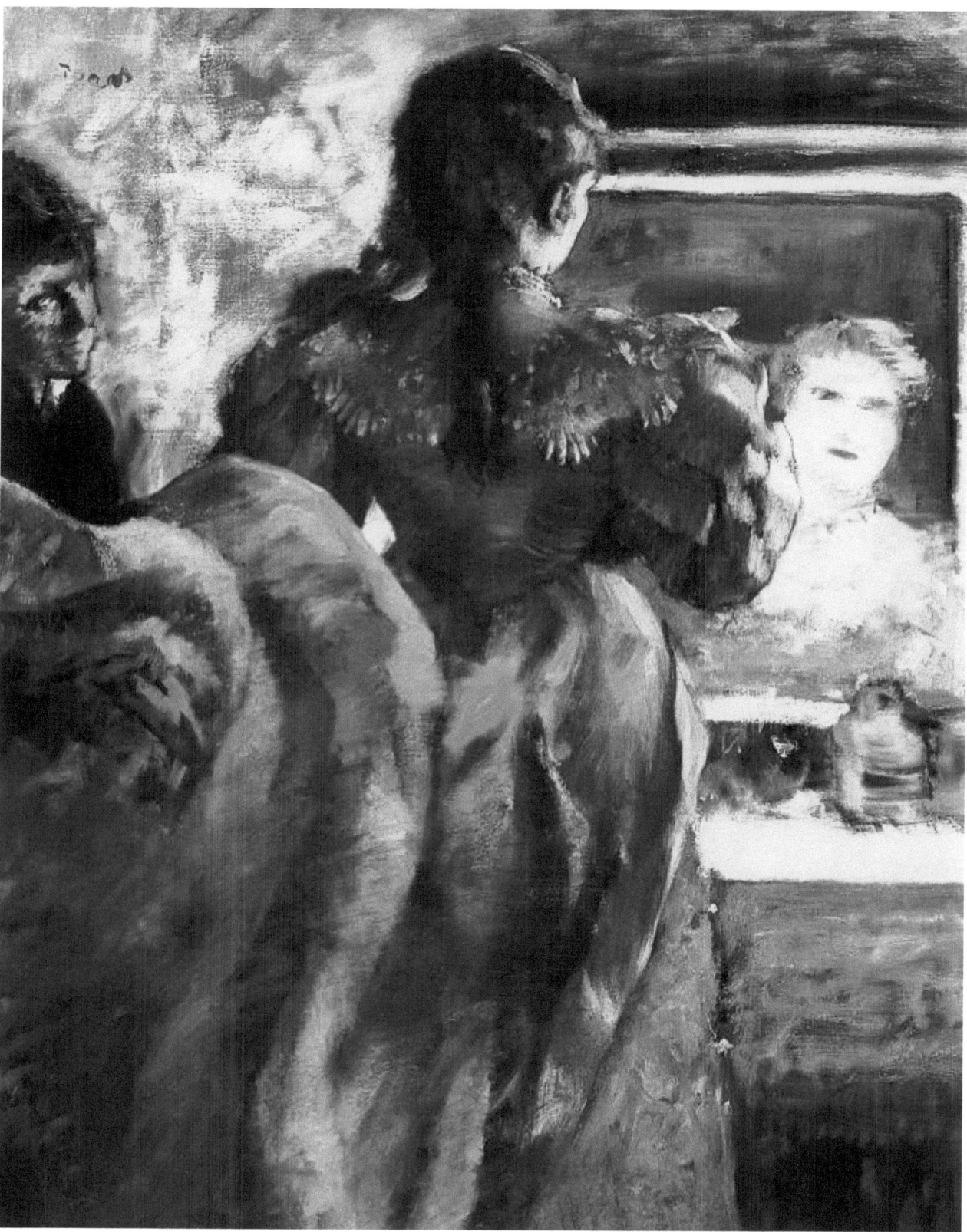

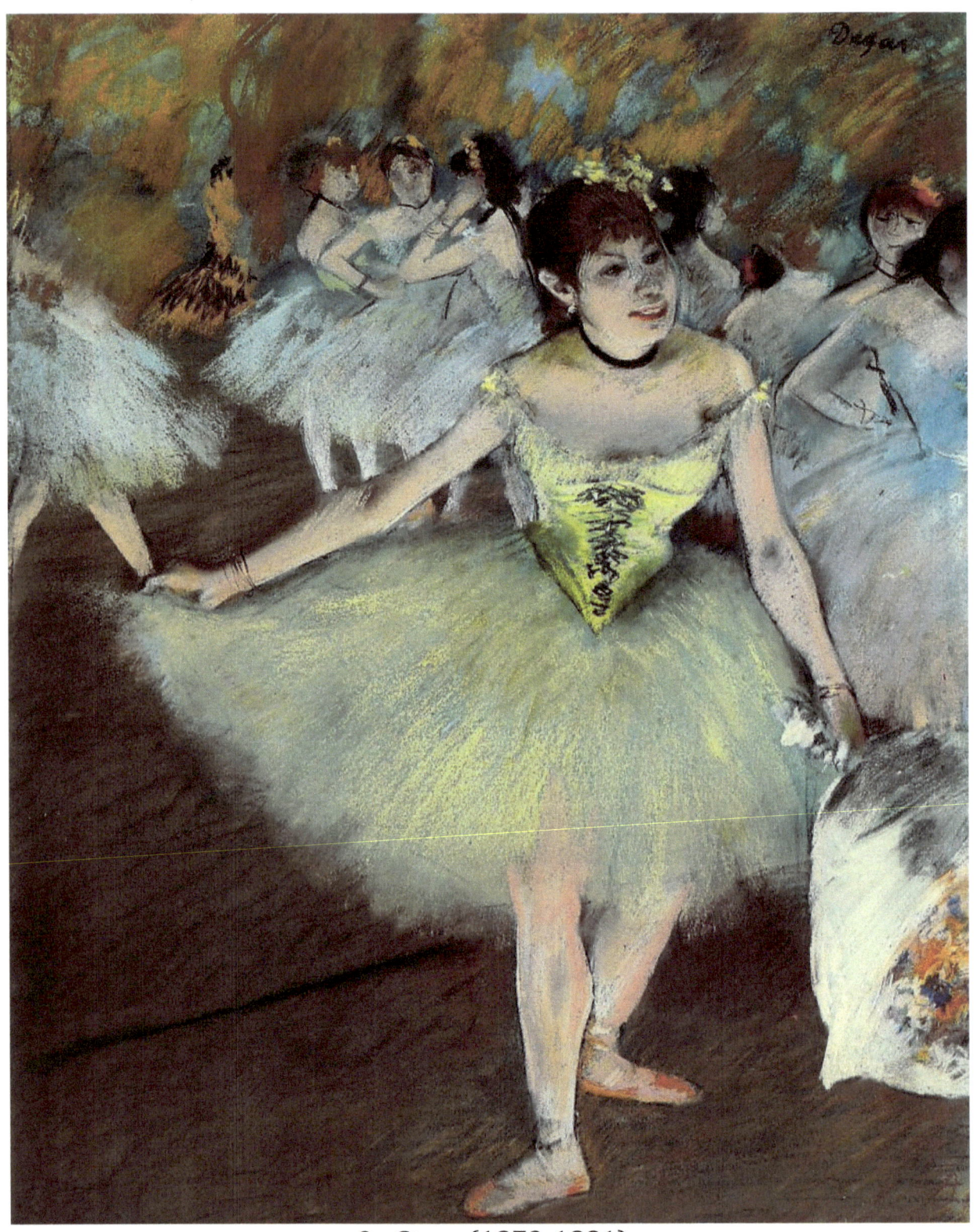

On Stage (1879-1881)
Edgar Degas

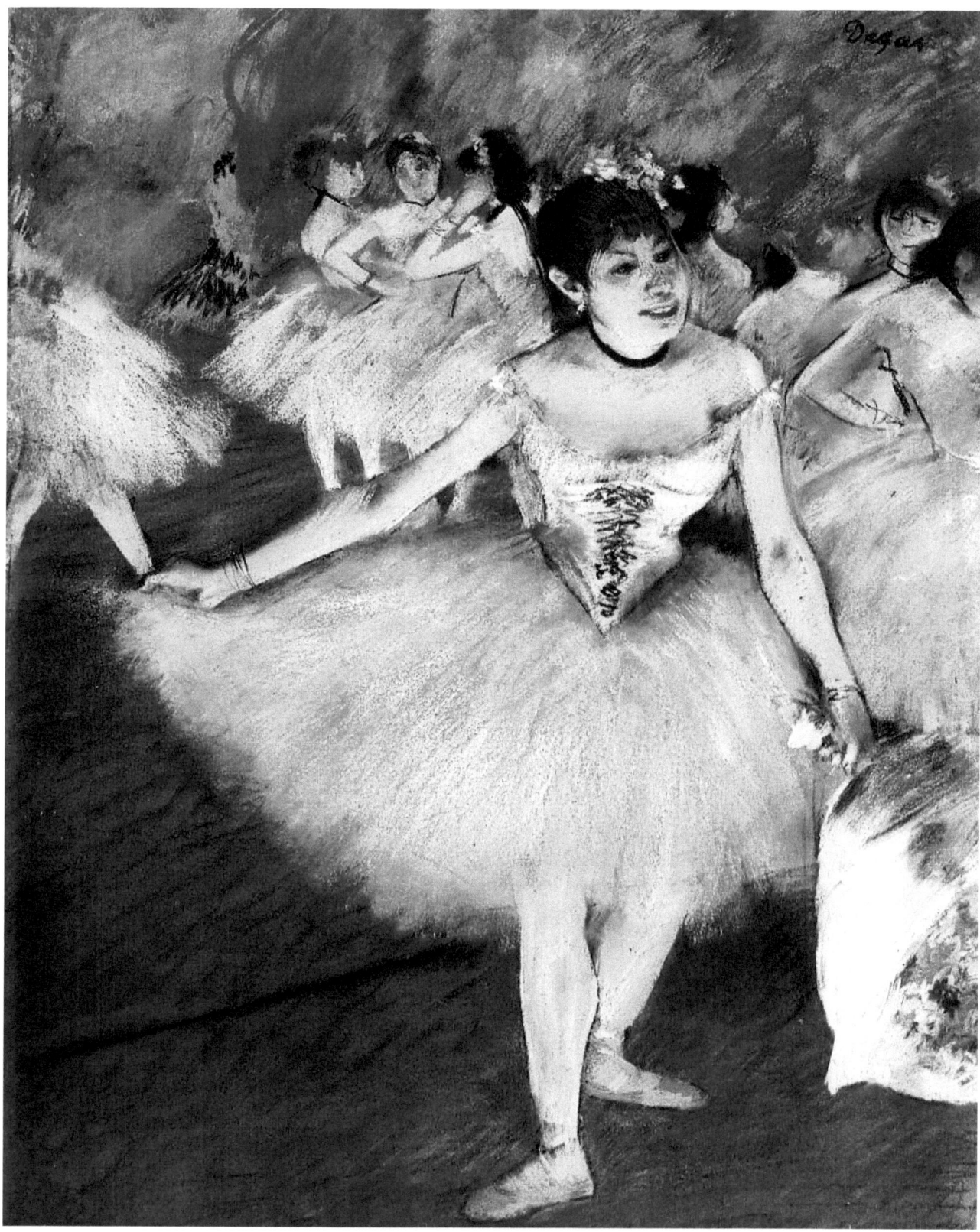

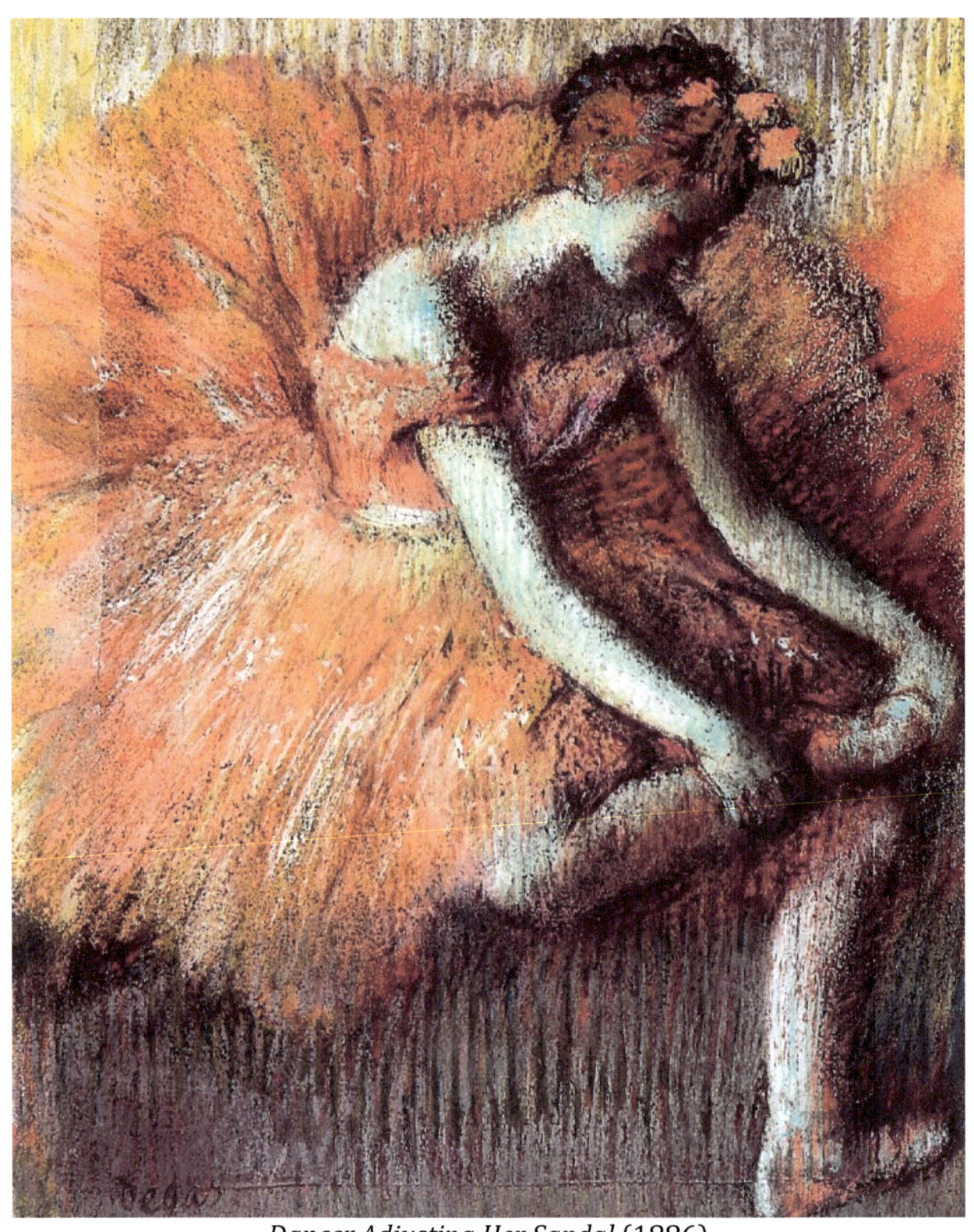

Dancer Adjusting Her Sandal (1886)
Edgar Degas

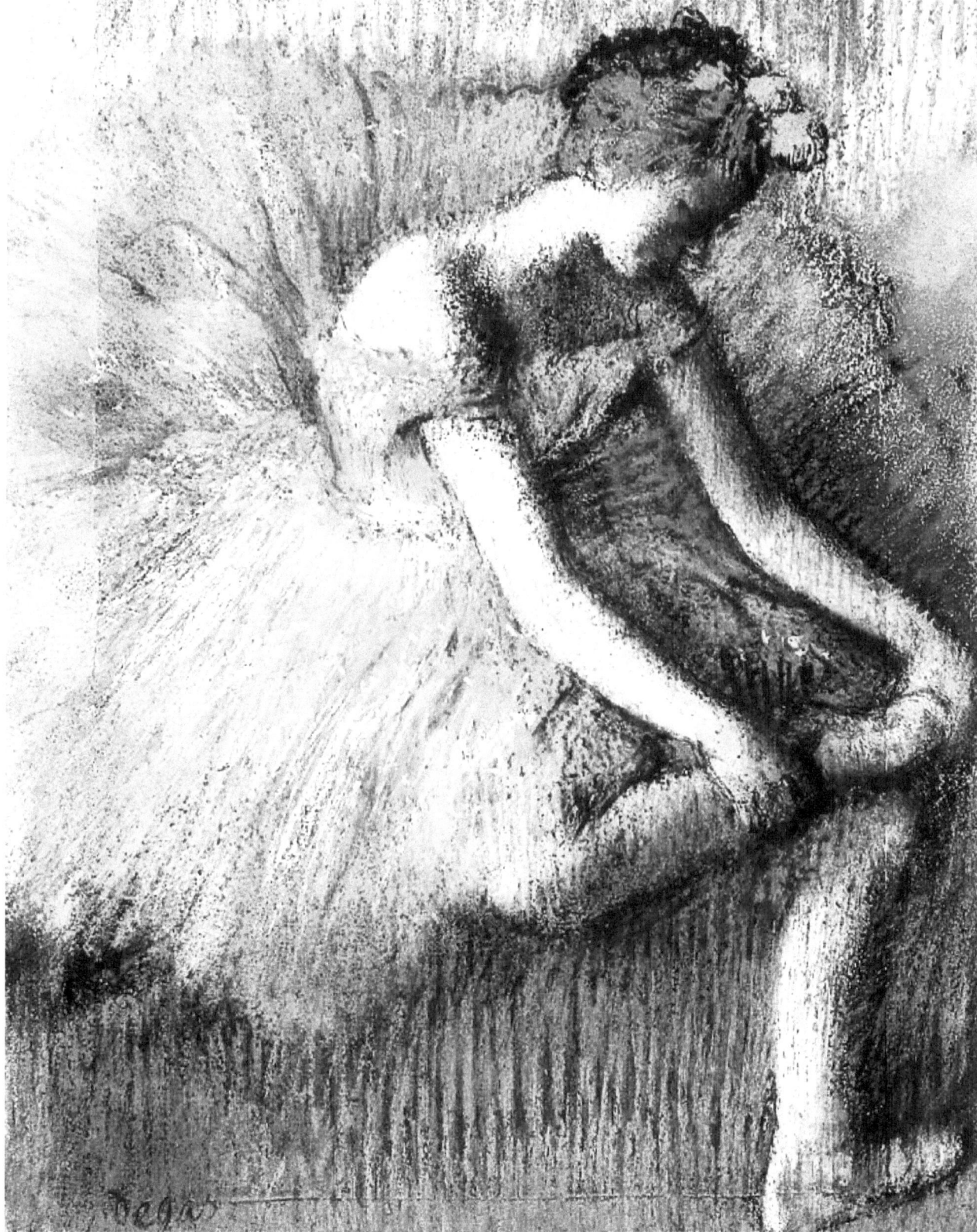

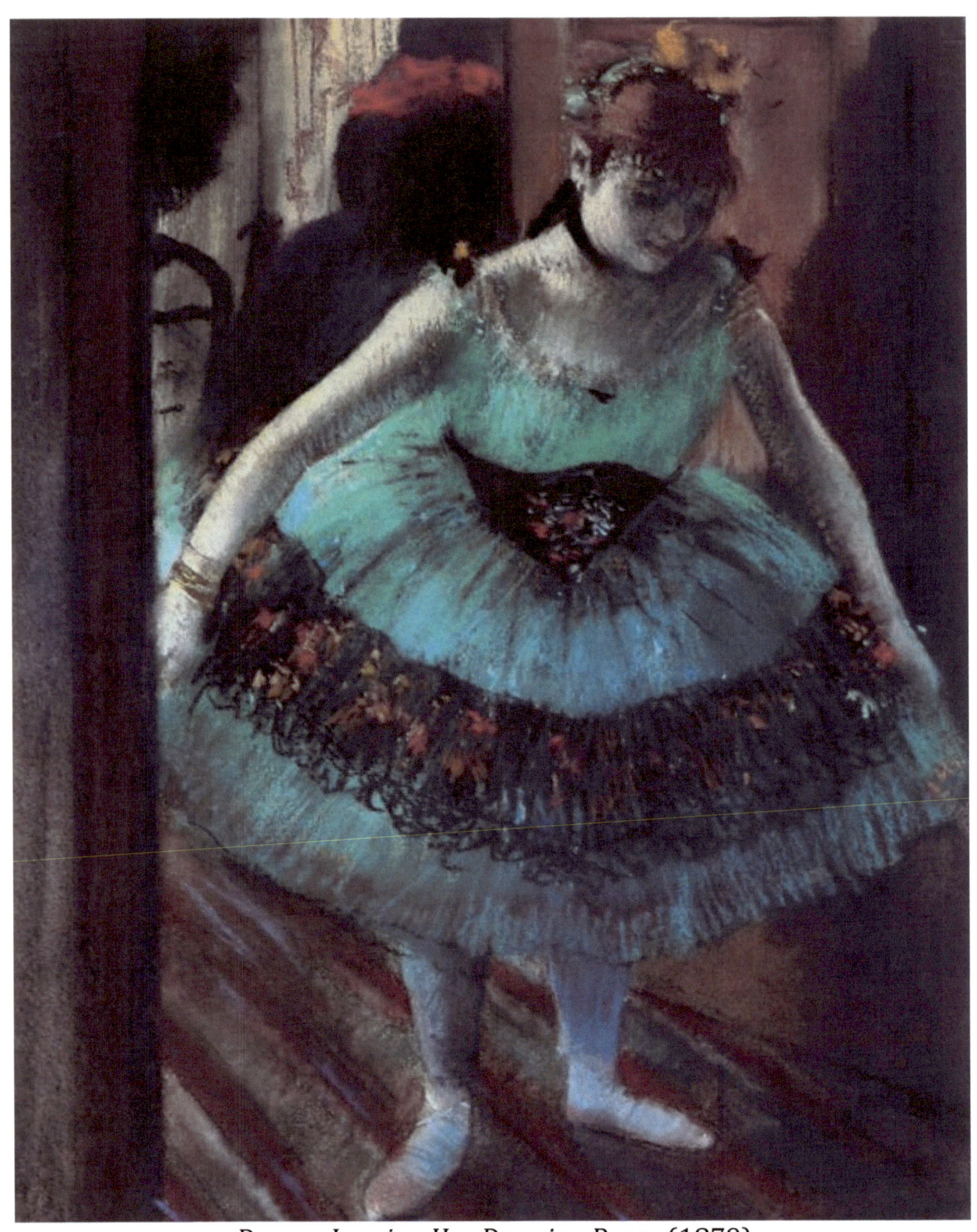

Dancer Leaving Her Dressing Room (1879)
Edgar Degas

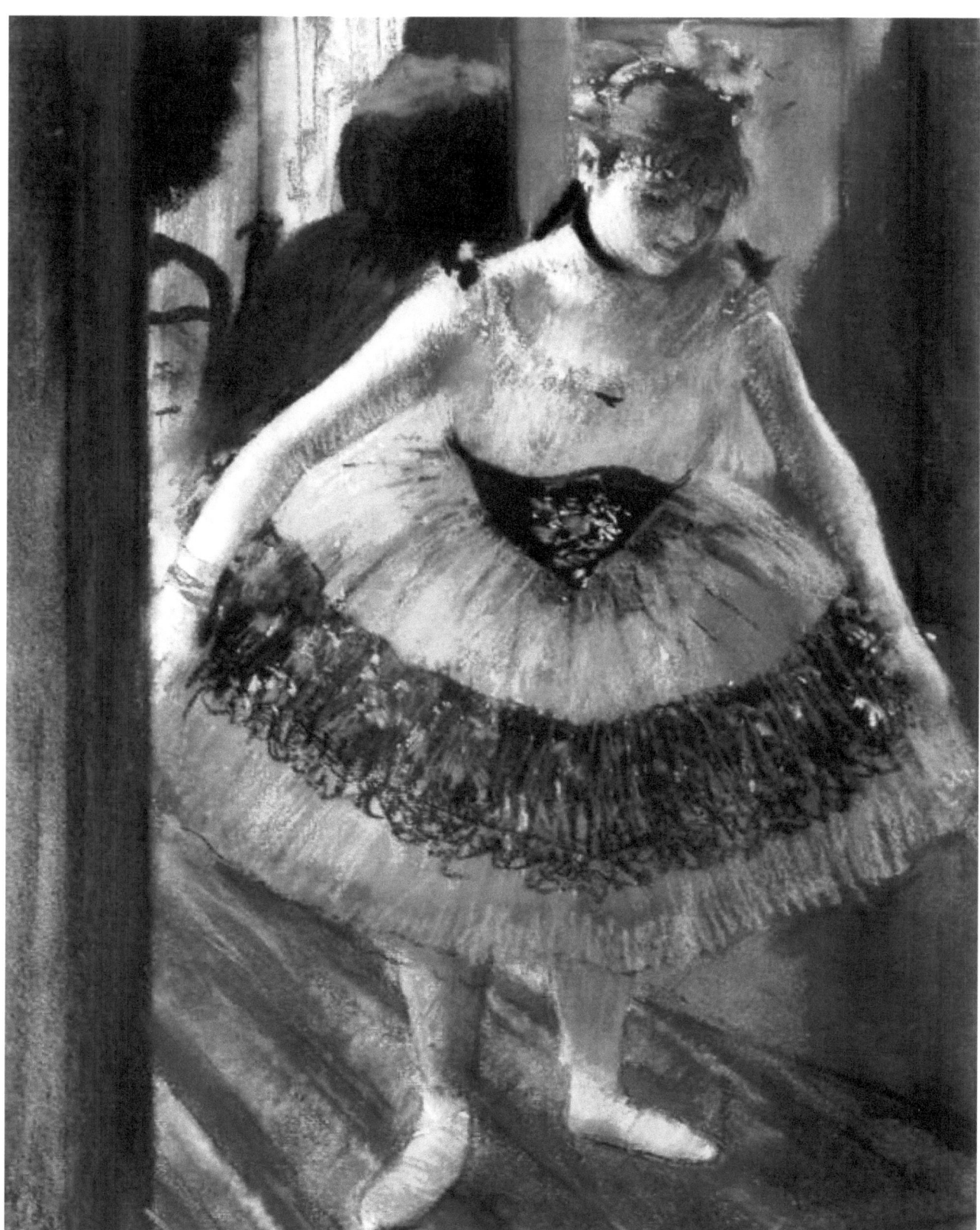

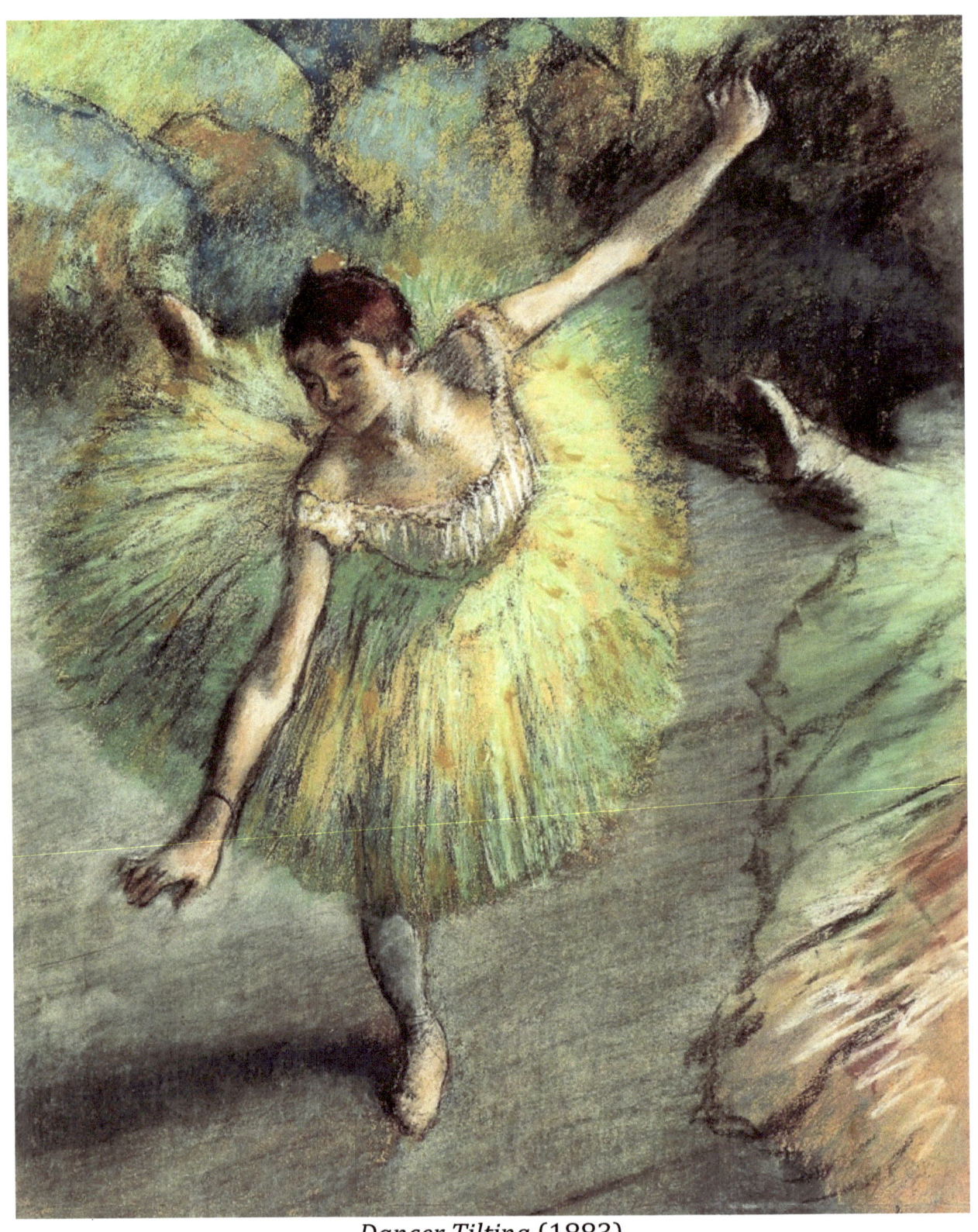

Dancer Tilting (1883)
Edgar Degas

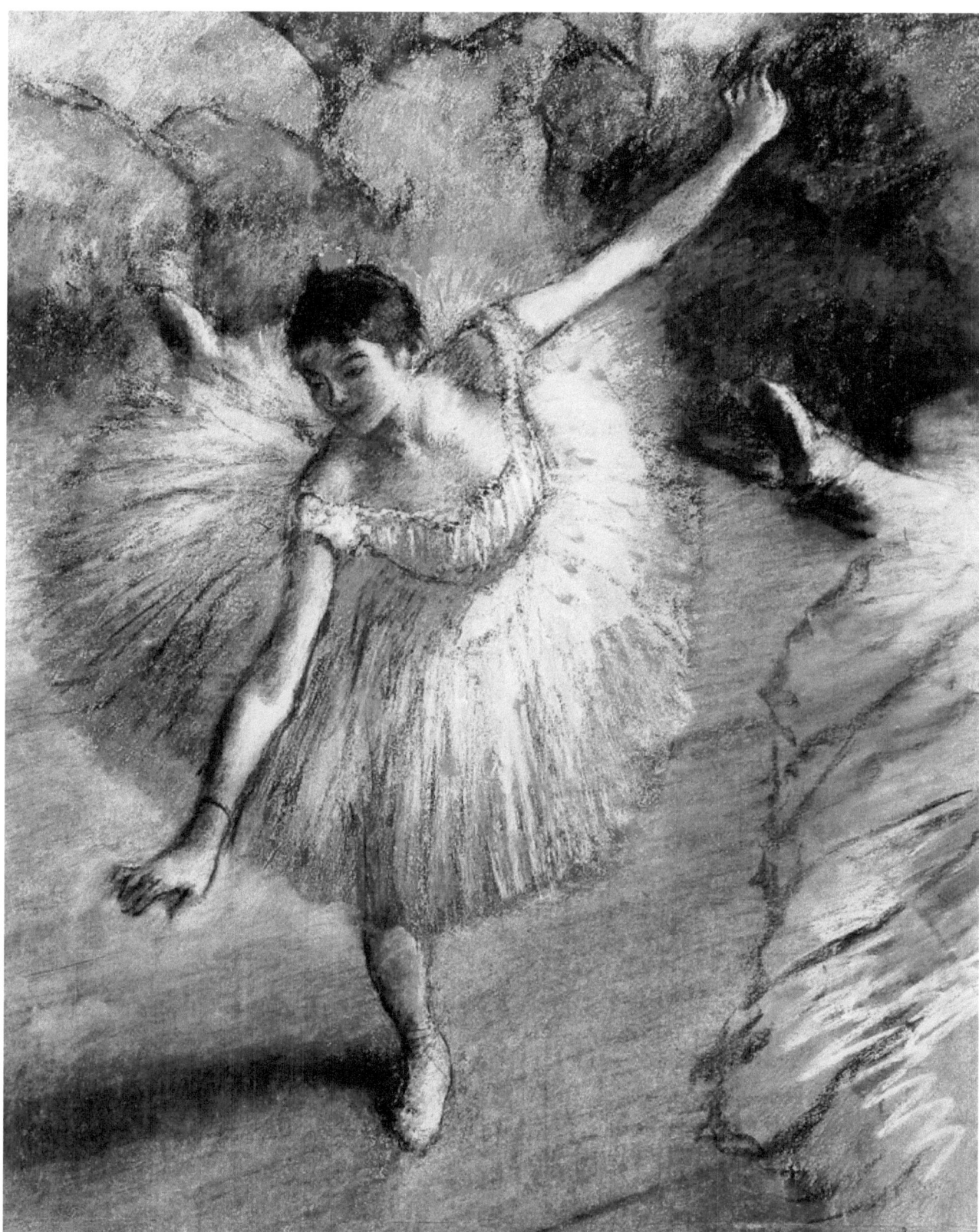

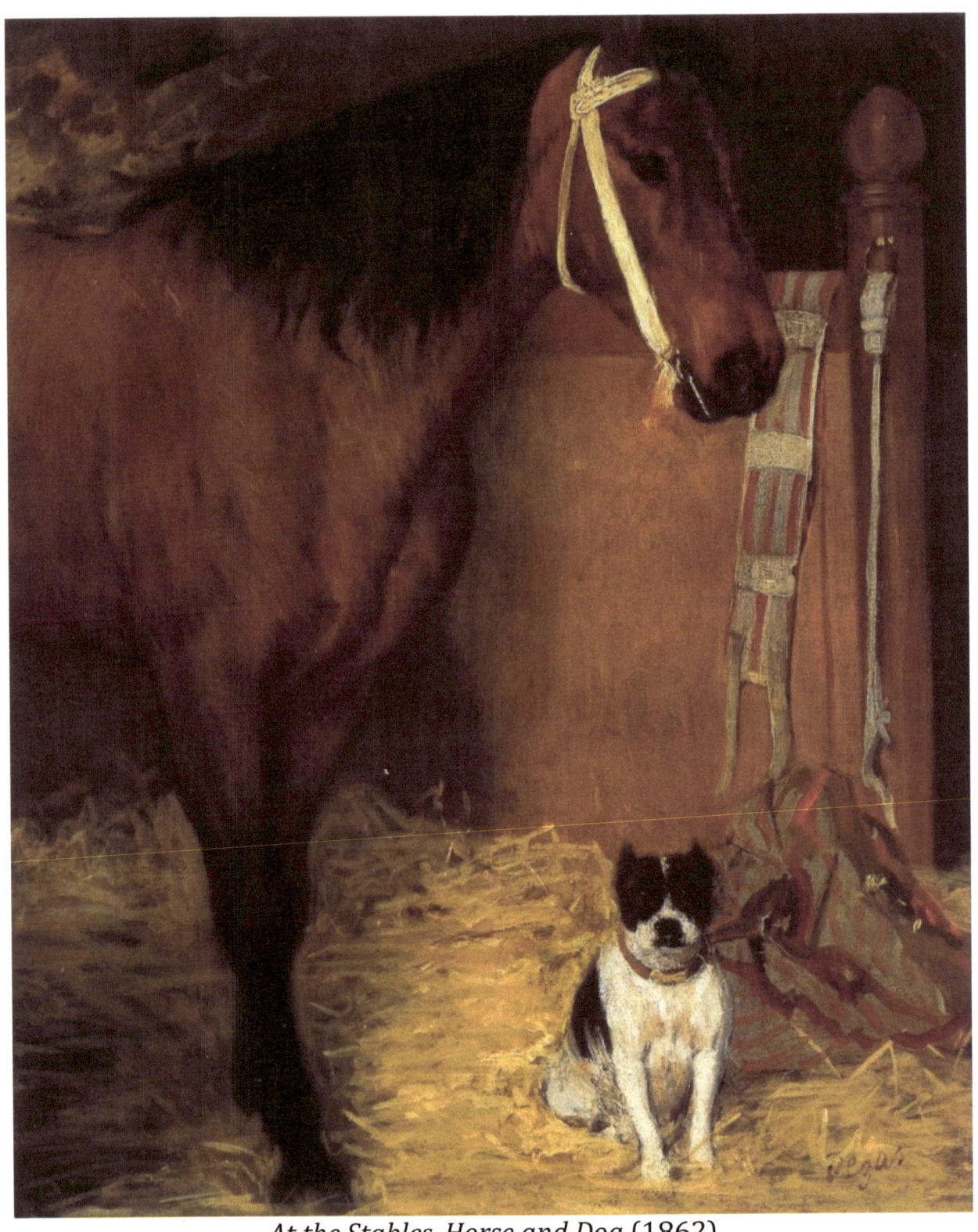

At the Stables, Horse and Dog (1862)
Edgar Degas

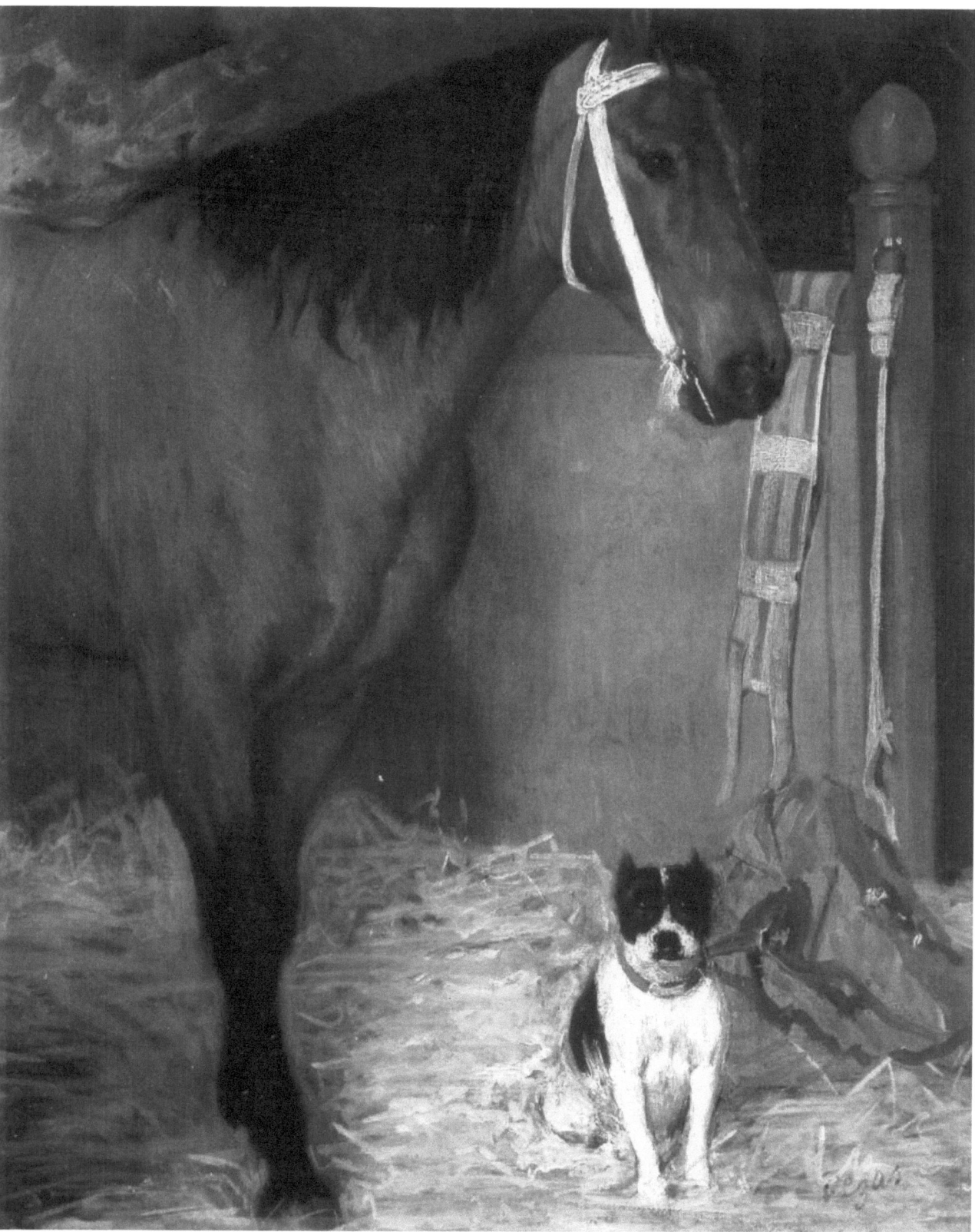

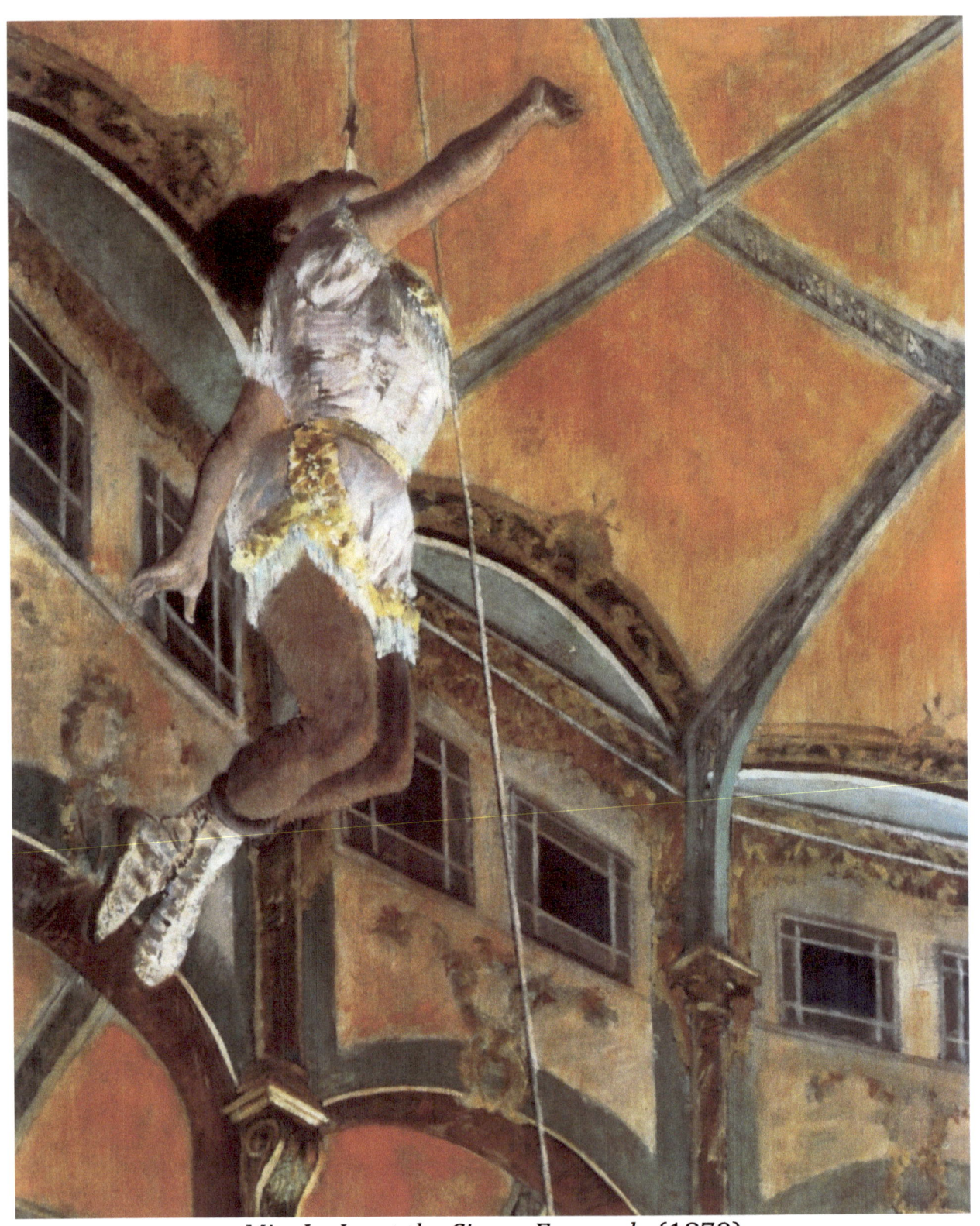

Miss La La at the Cirque Fernando (1879)
Edgar Degas

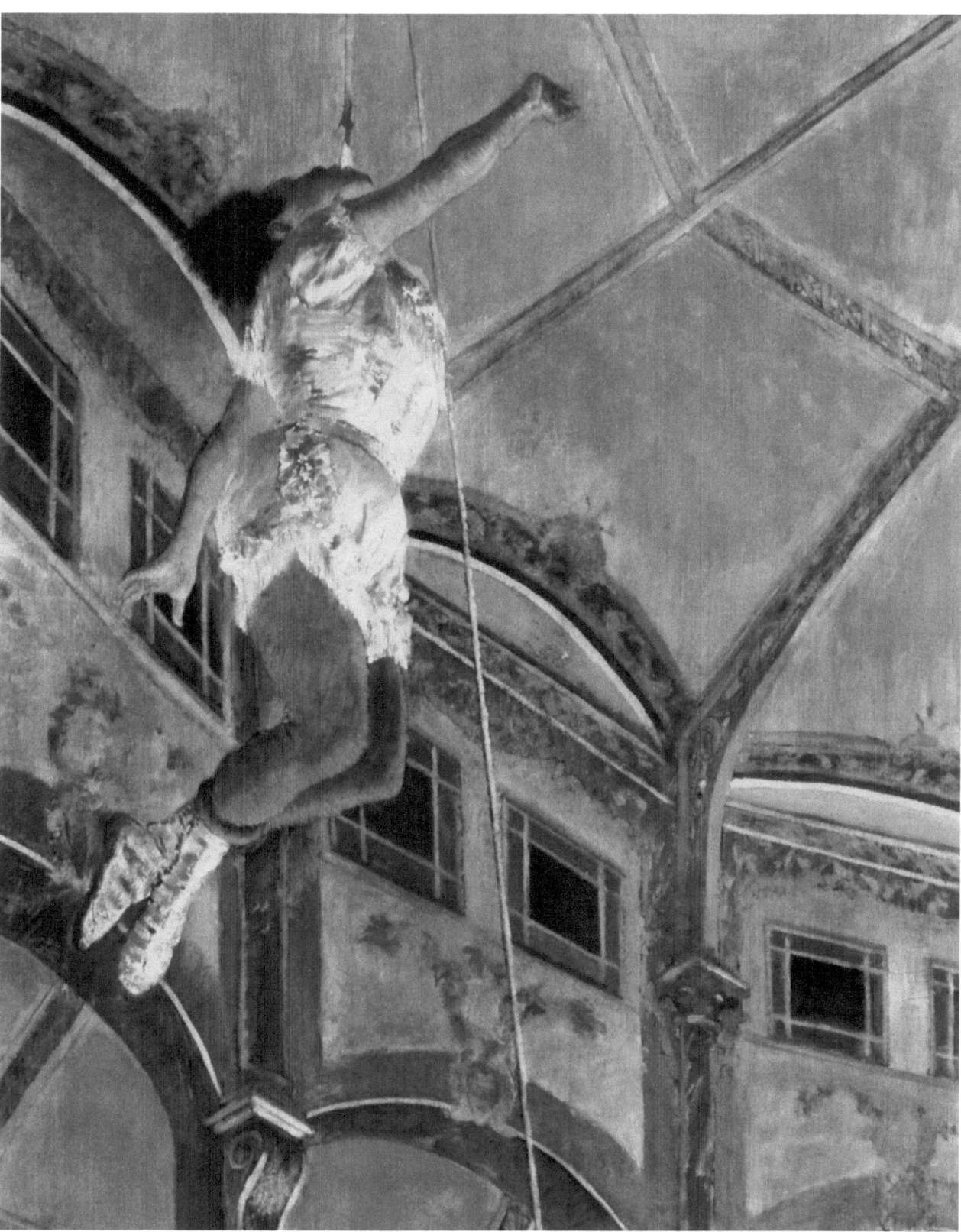

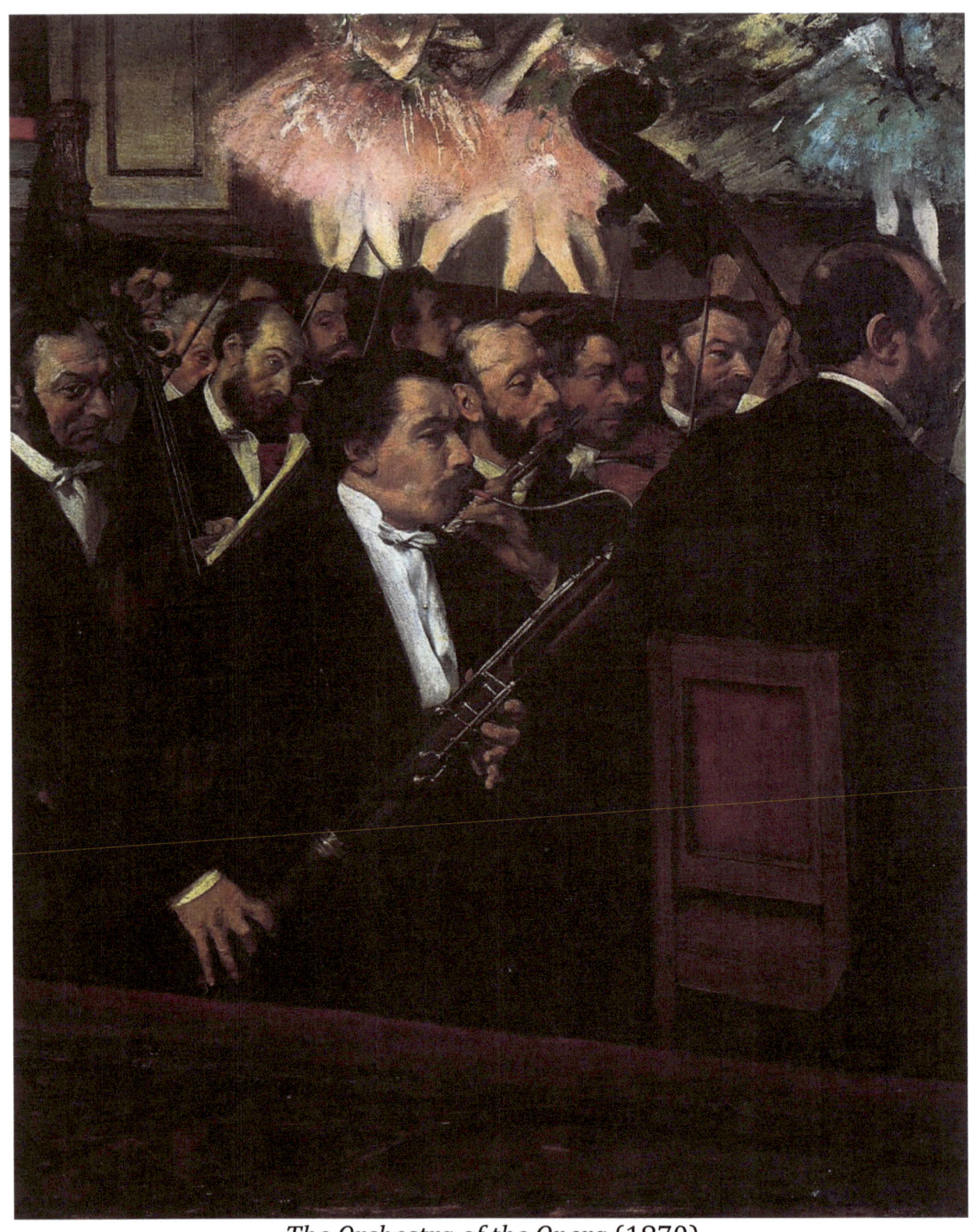

The Orchestra of the Opera (1870)
Edgar Degas

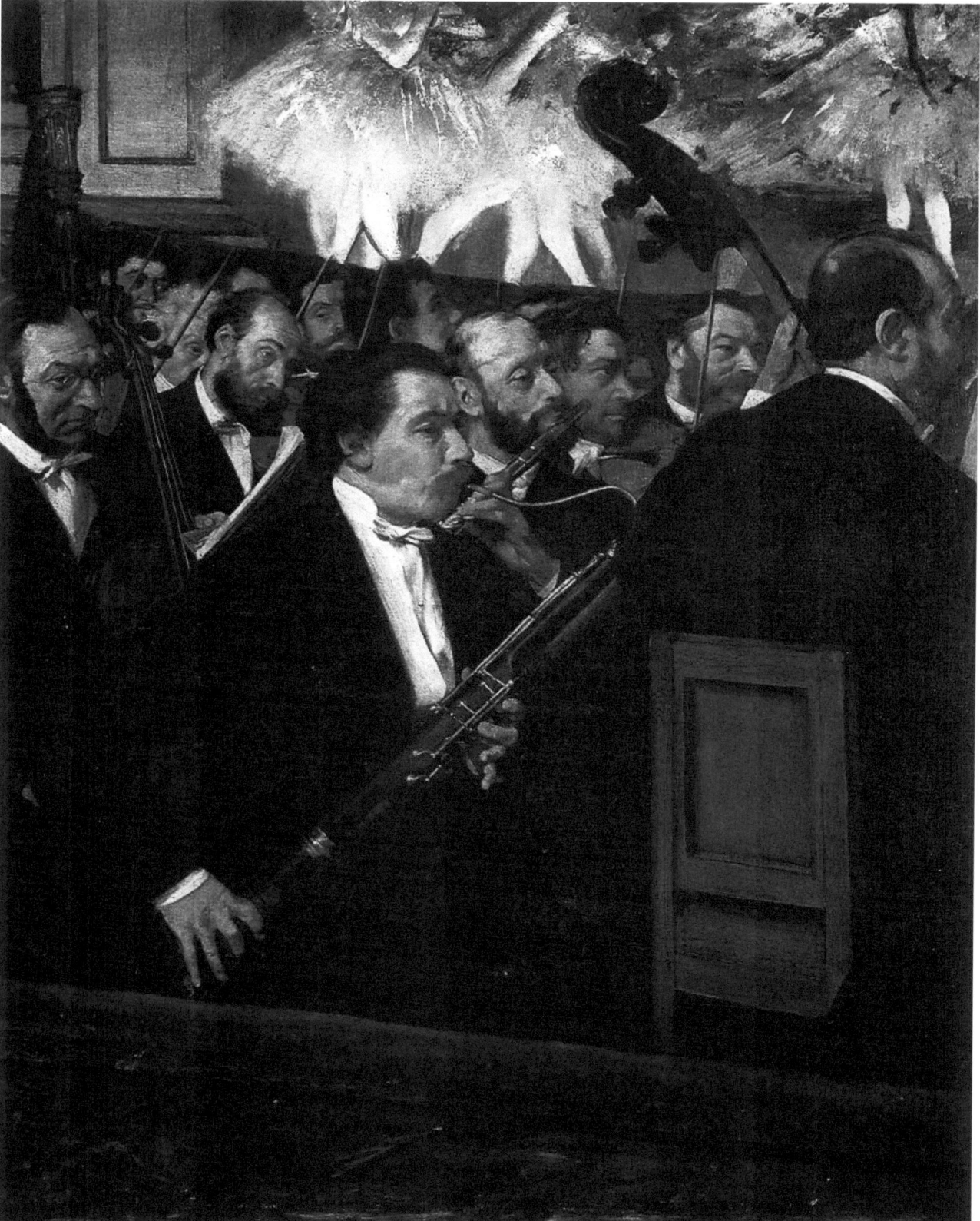

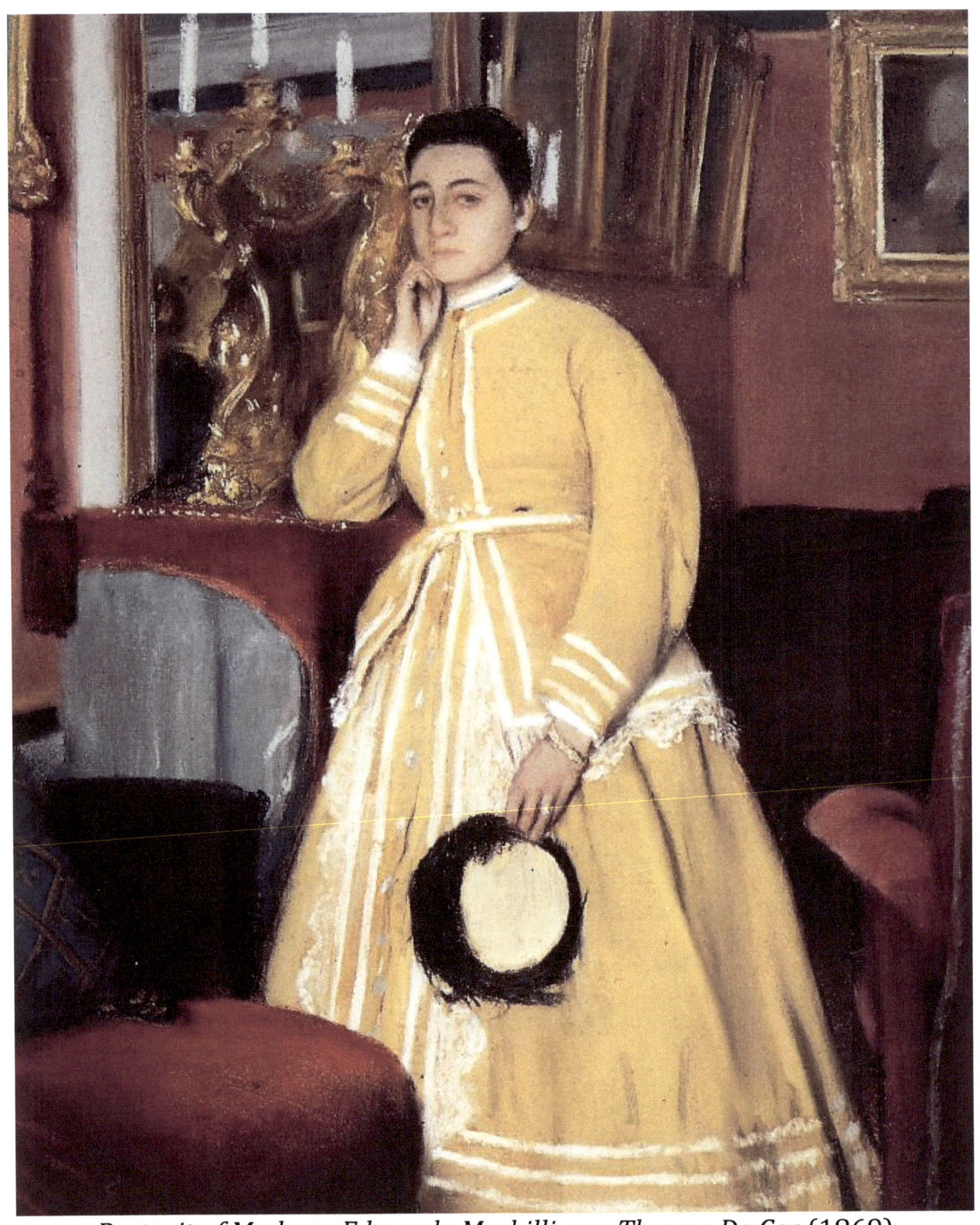

Portrait of Madame Edmondo Morbilli, nee Therese De Gas (1869)
Edgar Degas

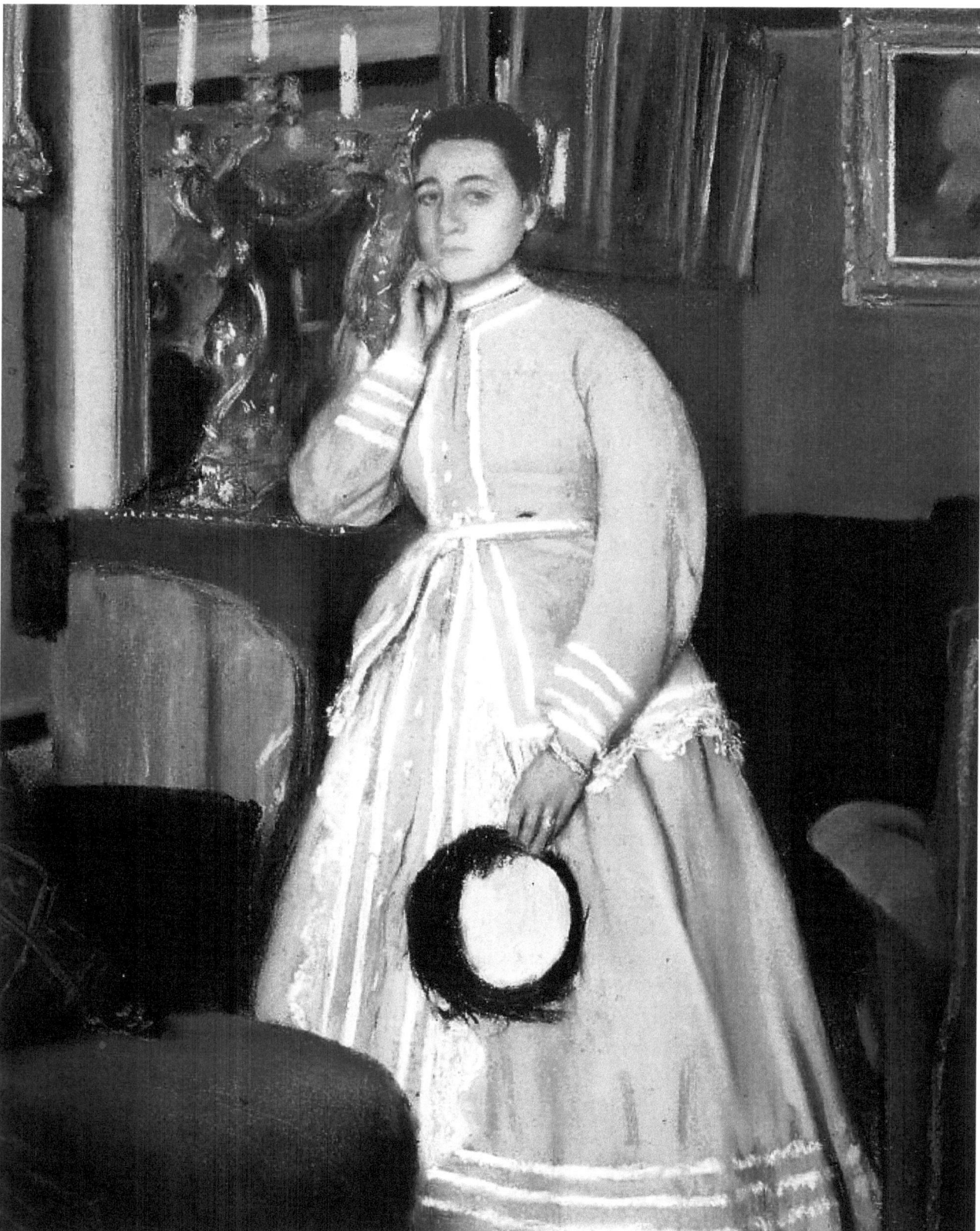

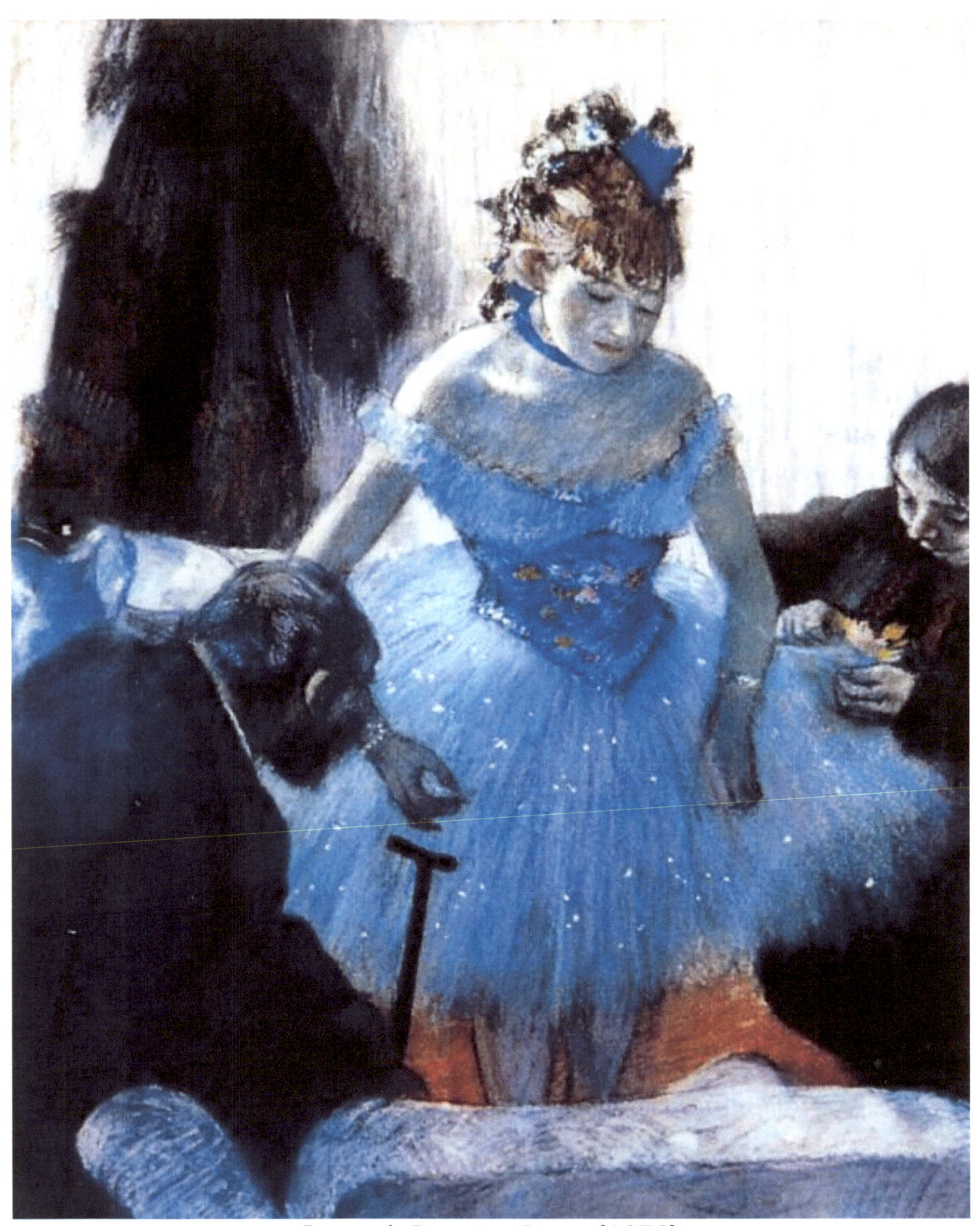

Dancer's Dressing Room (1878)
Edgar Degas

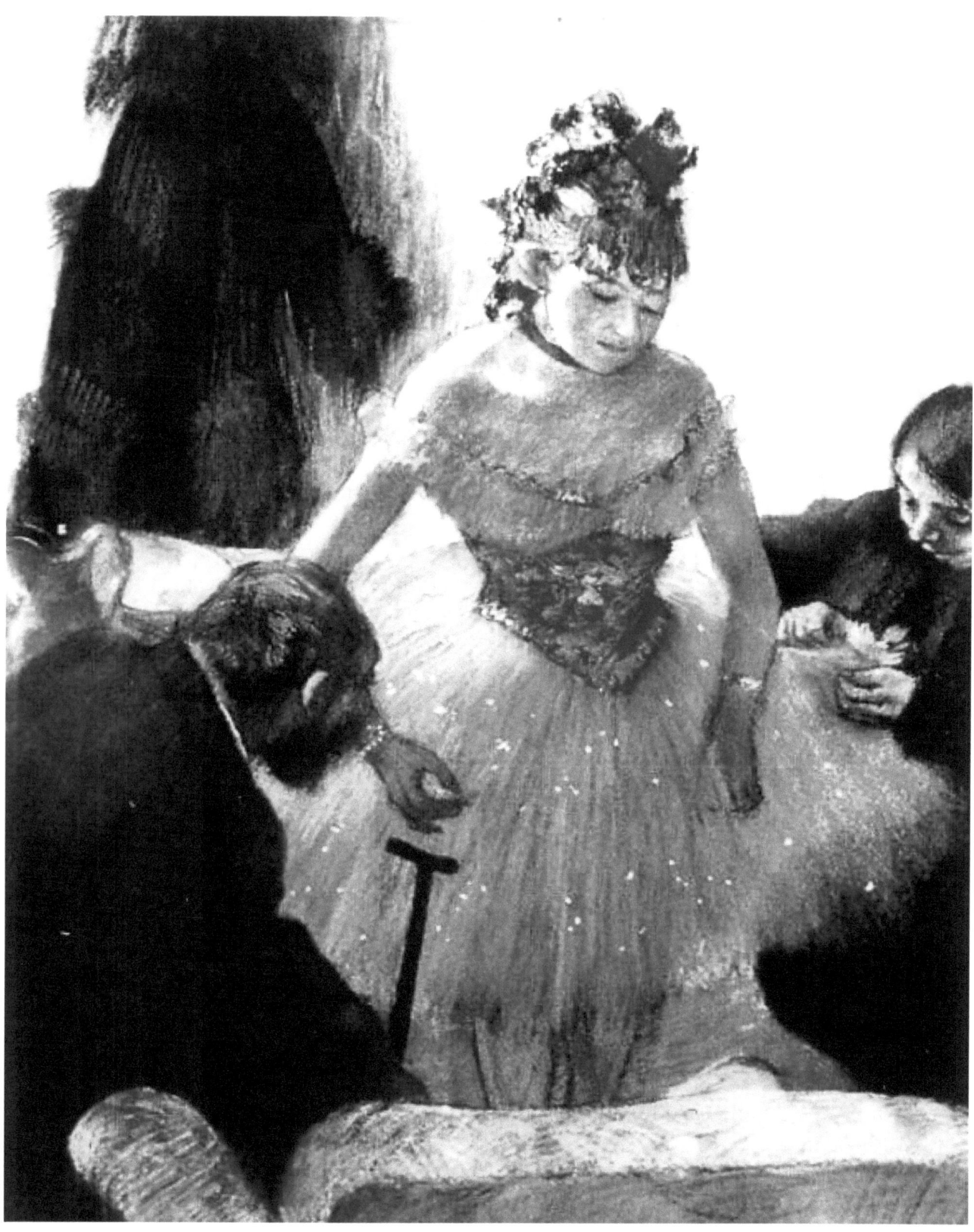

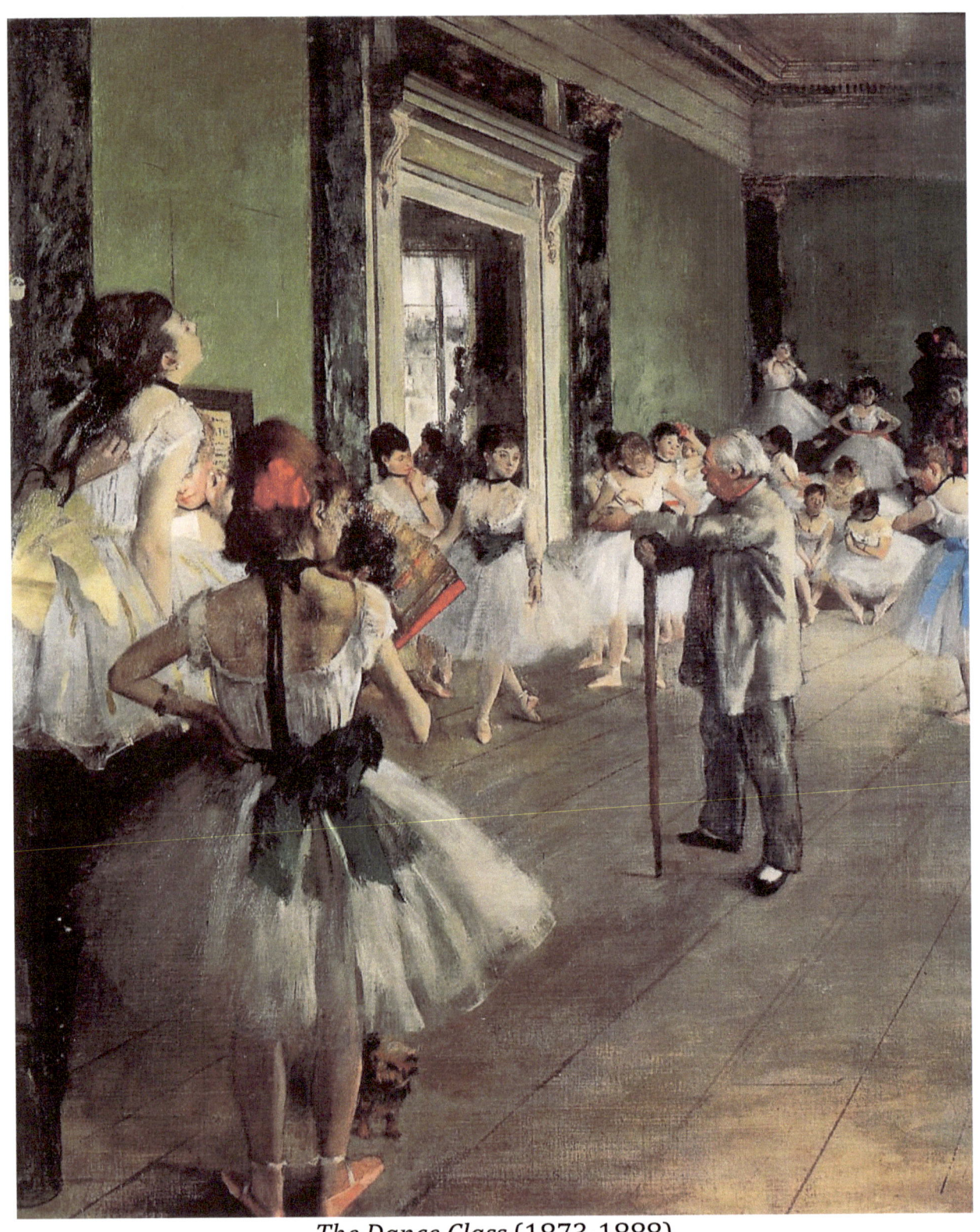

The Dance Class (1873-1888)
Edgar Degas

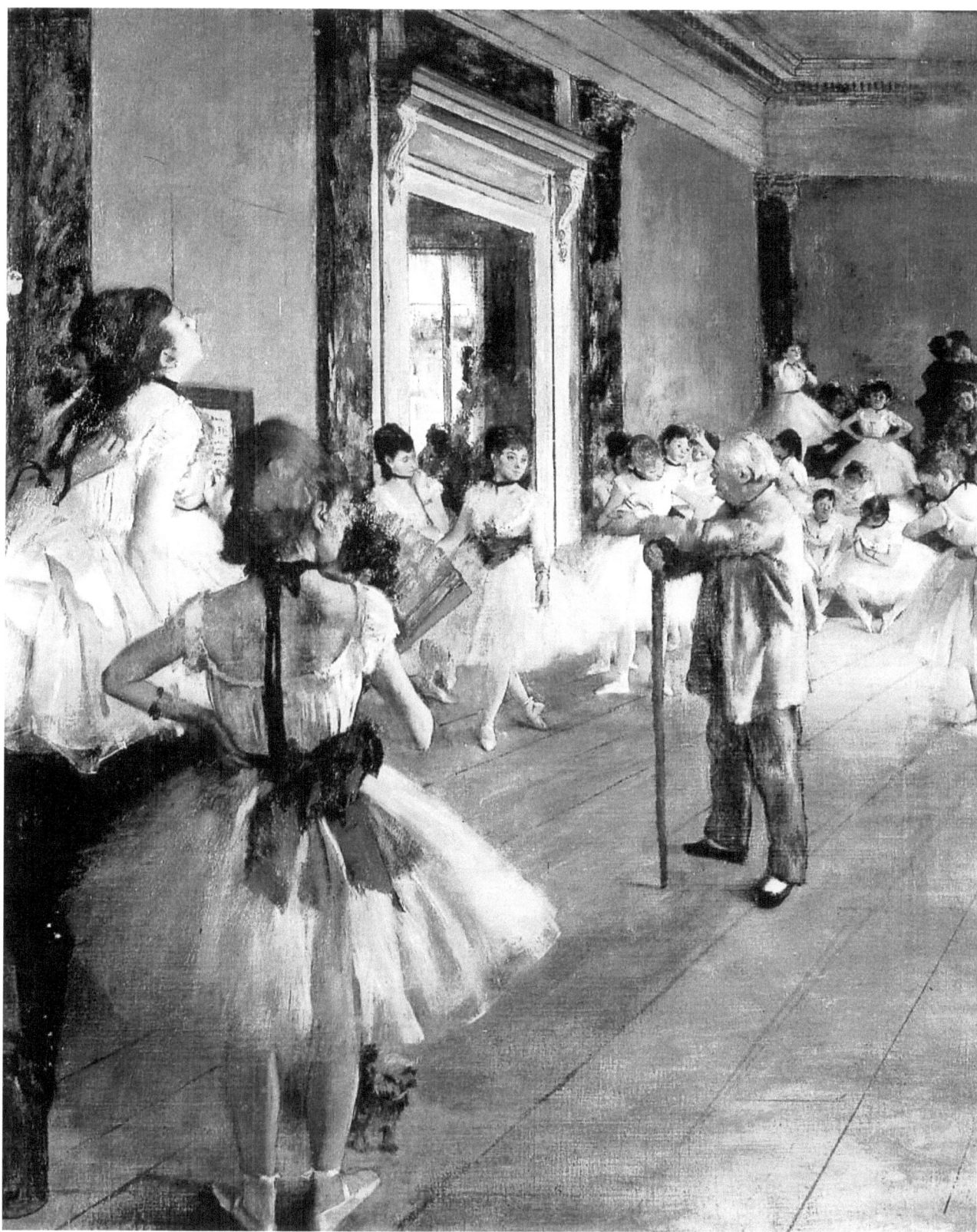

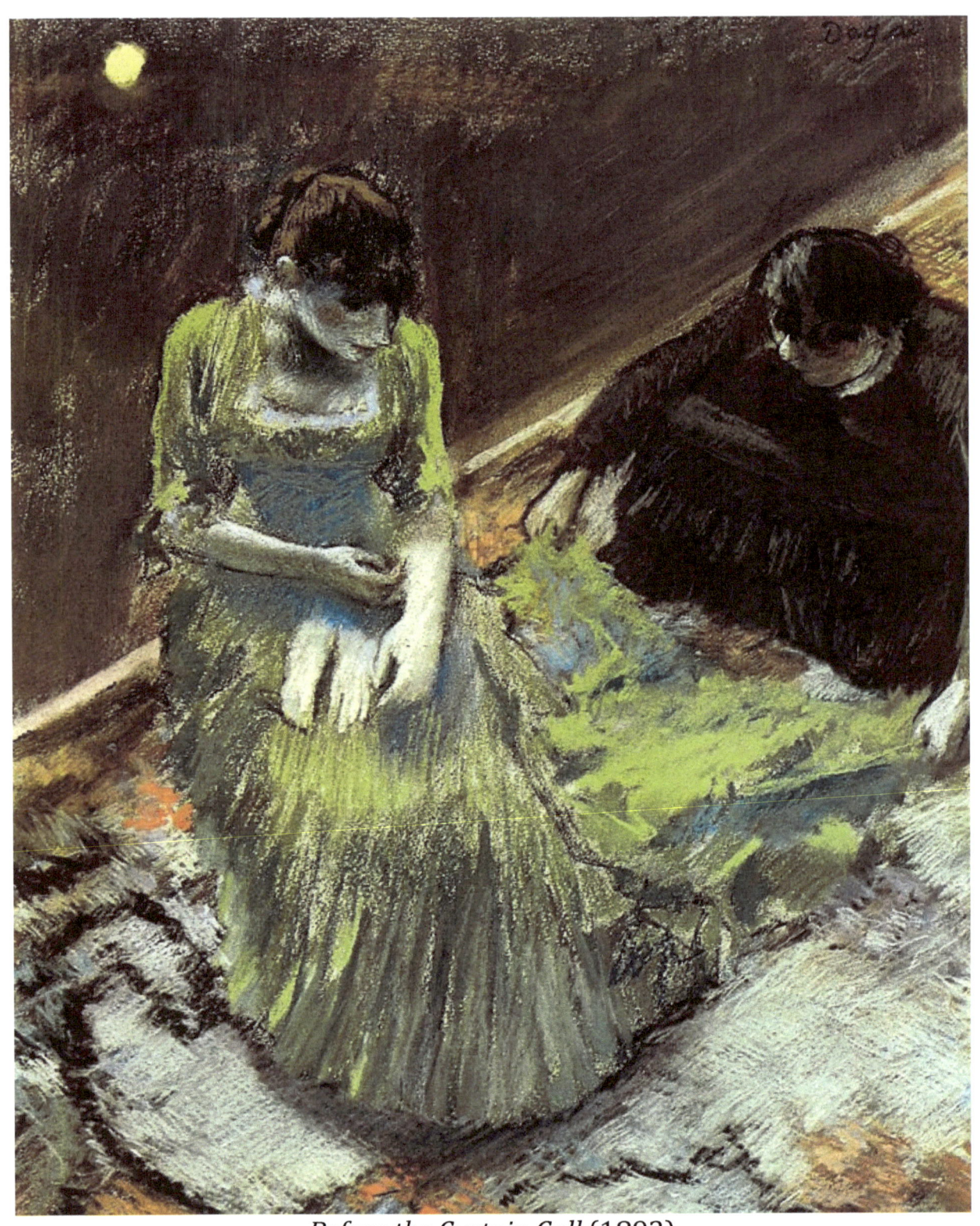

Before the Curtain Call (1892)
Edgar Degas

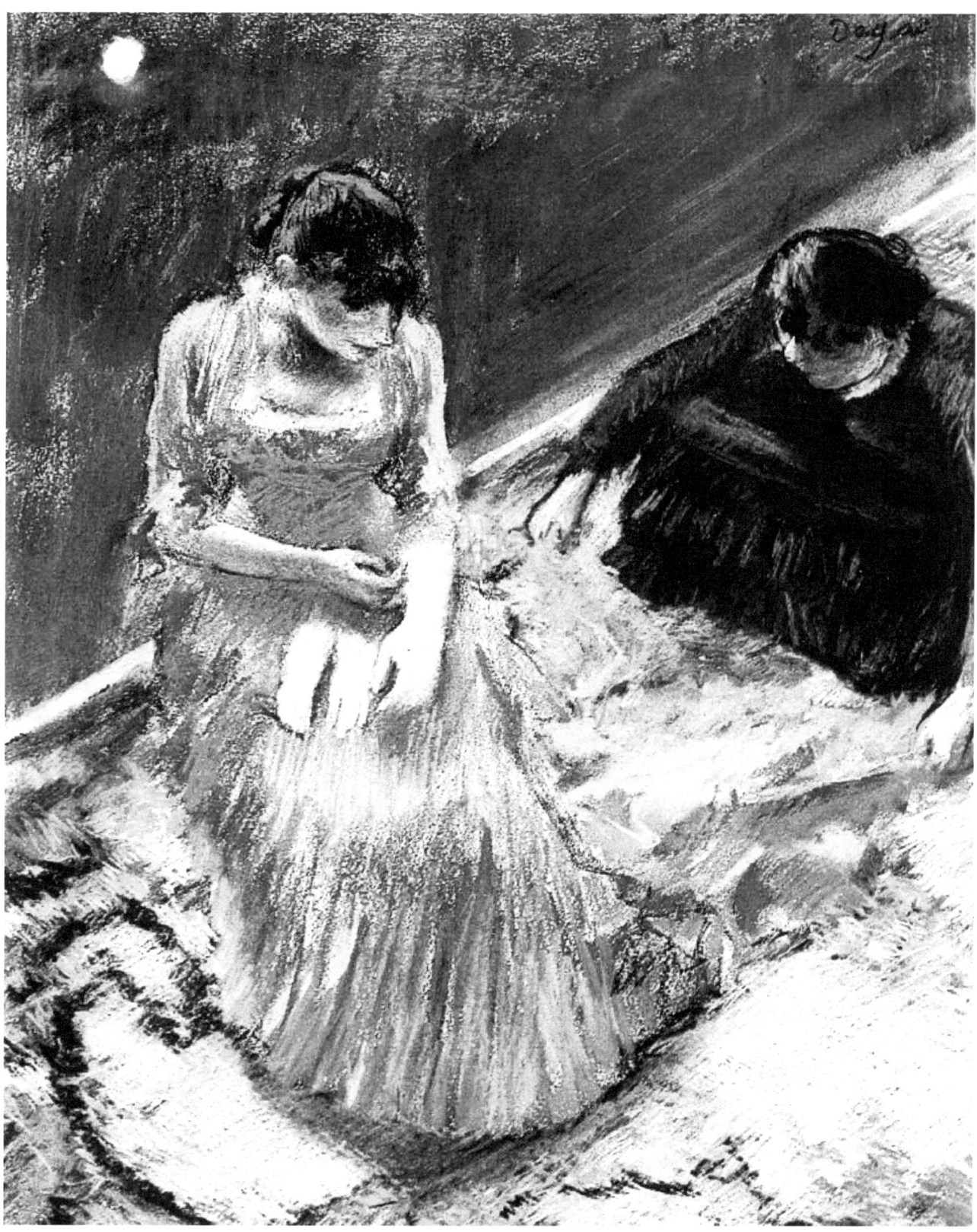

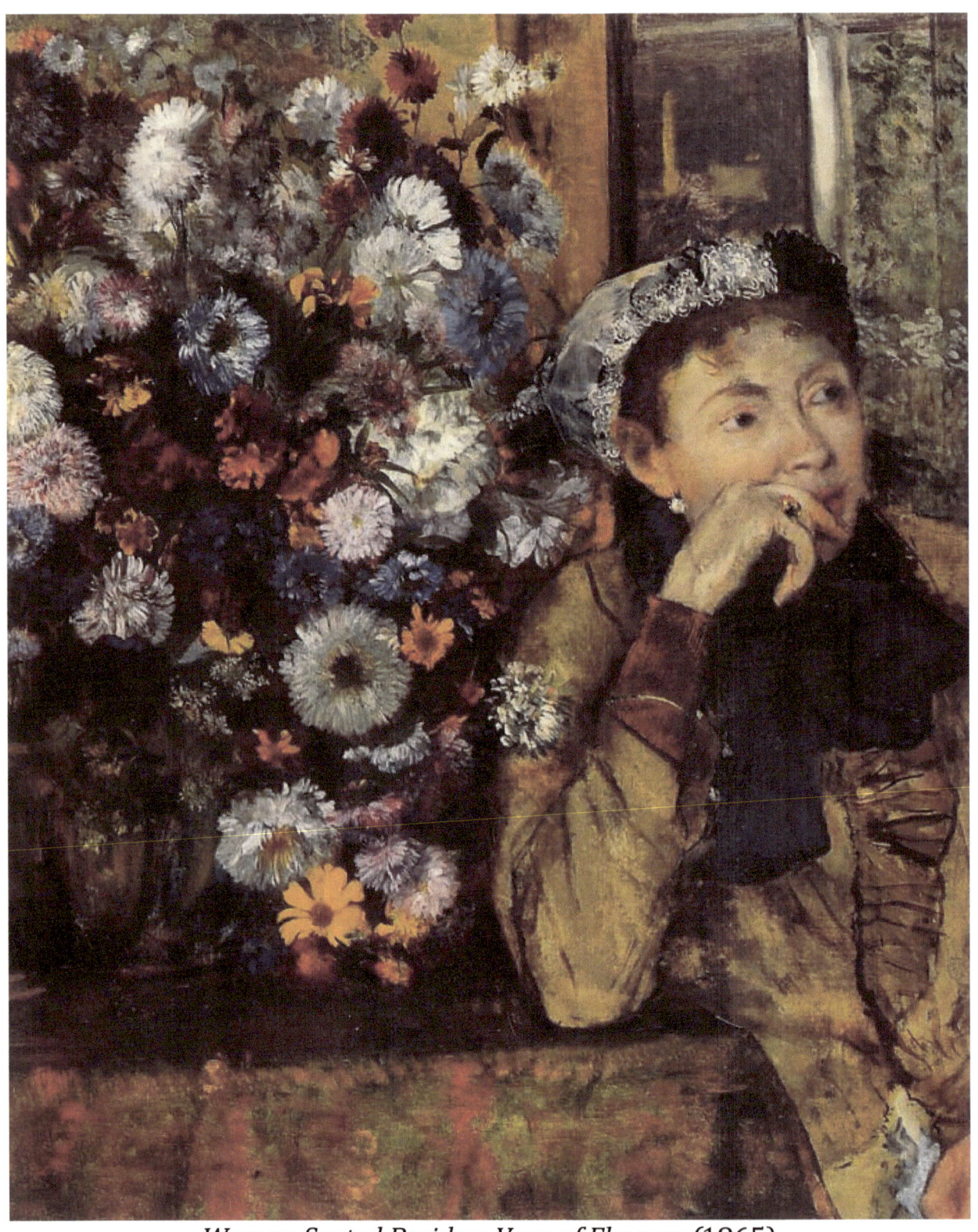

Woman Seated Beside a Vase of Flowers (1865)
Edgar Degas

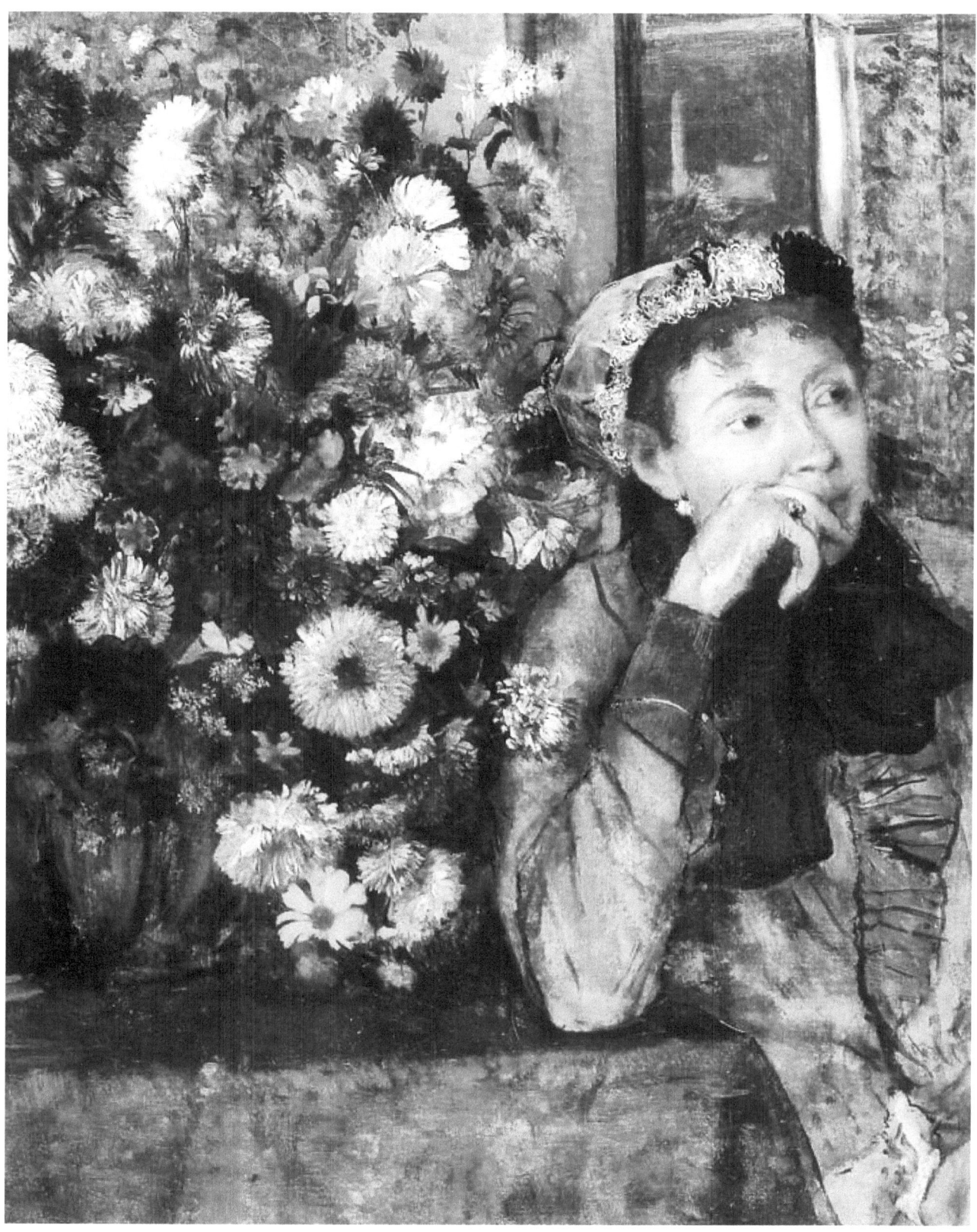

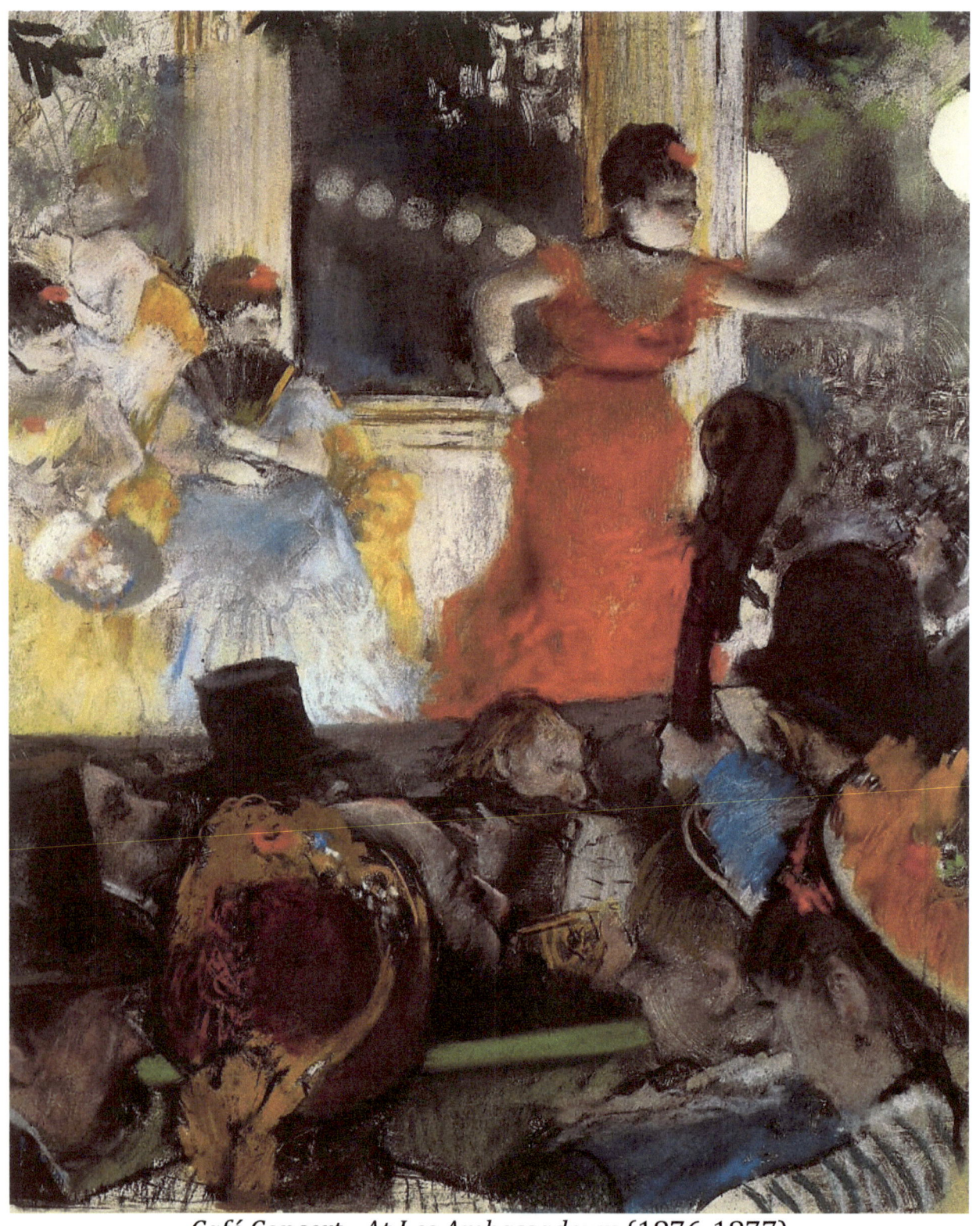

Café Concert - At Les Ambassadeurs (1876-1877)
Edgar Degas

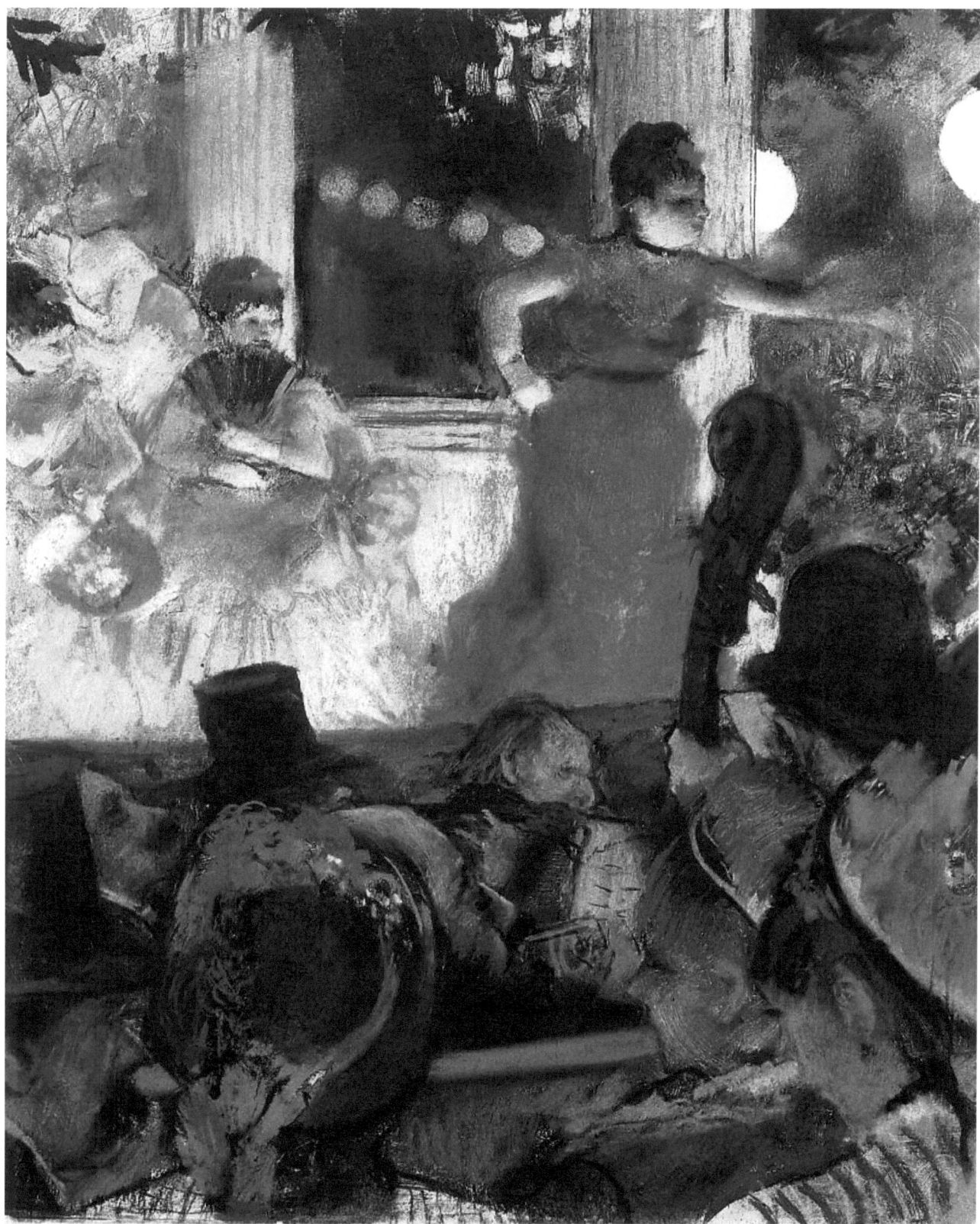

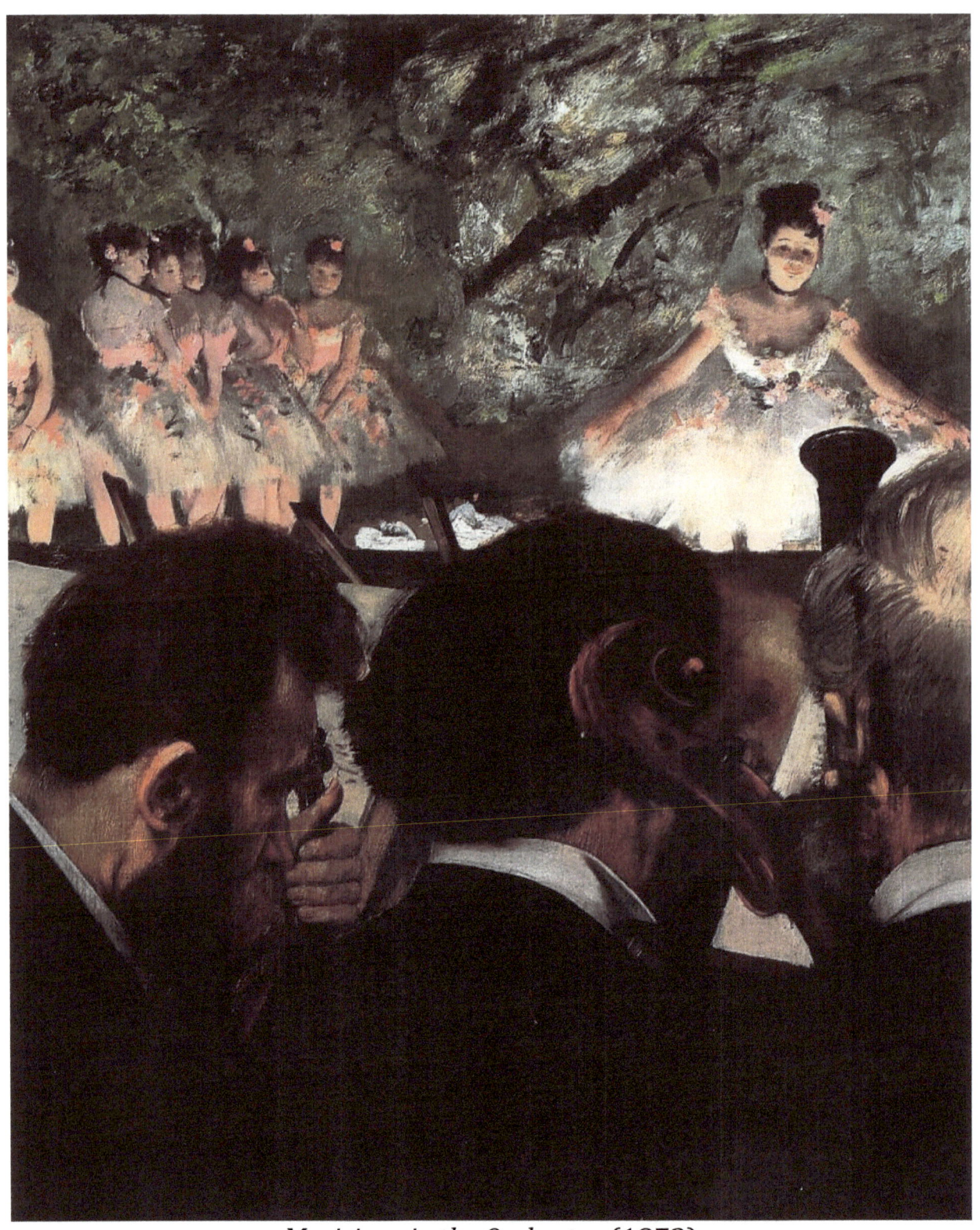

Musicians in the Orchestra (1872)
Edgar Degas

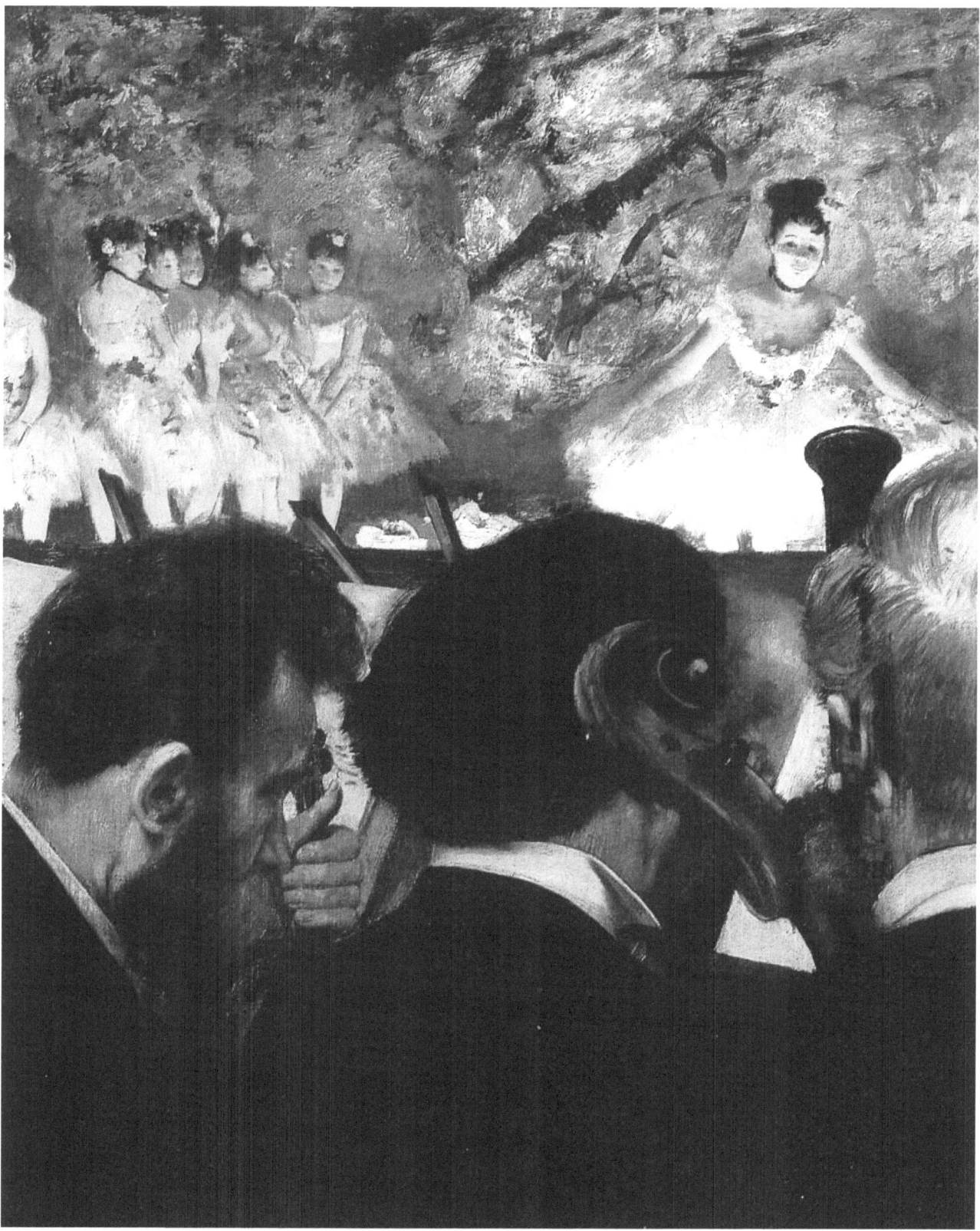